OPERANT CONDITIONING

A GUIDE TO SKINNERIAN PSYCHOLOGY

AF720627

TABLE OF CONTENTS

INTRODUCTION TO OPERANT CONDITIONING

Definition and Scope

Operant conditioning, a fundamental concept in behavioral psychology, refers to the process by which an individual's behavior is shaped and modified through reinforcement or punishment. Unlike classical conditioning, which focuses on involuntary responses to stimuli, operant conditioning centers on voluntary actions and their consequences. At the core of operant conditioning lies the principle that behaviors are influenced by their outcomes – that is, the rewards or punishments they elicit. By systematically examining the relationship between behavior and its subsequent effects, researchers and psychologists gain insights into the mechanisms underlying human and animal behavior.

One defining feature of operant conditioning is its emphasis on the role of reinforcement and punishment in shaping behavior. Reinforcement, whether in the form of positive rewards or the removal of negative stimuli, serves to strengthen and increase the likelihood of a specific behavior occurring again. Conversely, punishment, whether through the application of aversive consequences or the withdrawal of positive stimuli, aims to weaken and decrease the occurrence of a particular behavior. This dynamic interplay between reinforcement and punishment forms the basis of behavior modification, as individuals learn to associate their actions with favorable or unfavorable outcomes.

Operant conditioning extends beyond simple cause-and-effect relationships to encompass the concept of contingency, wherein the presentation of a consequence is contingent upon the occurrence of a specific behavior. This contingent relationship between behavior and its consequences highlights the predictability and determinism inherent in operant learning processes. As individuals navigate their environment and interact with stimuli, they continually encounter opportunities to engage in behaviors that yield desirable outcomes while avoiding those that lead to adverse consequences.

Drawing from the pioneering work of B.F. Skinner and other influential researchers, operant conditioning has found application across diverse domains, including education, parenting, organizational behavior, and clinical intervention. Its capacity to elucidate the behavioral dynamics governing human and animal conduct has positioned operant conditioning as a cornerstone of modern psychological understanding. By unraveling the intricacies of how behaviors are influenced and maintained, operant conditioning offers invaluable insights and practical implications for promoting positive change and adaptive behavior in individuals and communities.

Fundamental Differences Between Classical and Operant Conditioning

Classical conditioning, initially studied by Ivan Pavlov, focuses on the association between a neutral stimulus and an involuntary response. This form of learning occurs through the process of stimulus substitution, whereby the neutral stimulus becomes a conditioned stimulus capable of evoking the same response as the unconditioned stimulus. In contrast, operant conditioning, pioneered by B. F. Skinner, emphasizes the relationship between a voluntary behavior and its consequences. Rather than focusing on reflexive responses, operant conditioning is concerned with the modification of behaviors based on their outcomes. One of the fundamental distinctions between the two types of conditioning lies in the nature of the target behavior. In classical conditioning, the emphasis is placed on eliciting a reflexive response, while operant conditioning aims to modify and control voluntary actions. Another key difference involves the role of the individual's agency in operant conditioning, where the subject actively engages in behaviors that are then shaped by their consequences. In classical conditioning, the response occurs passively, triggered by the environmental stimuli. Moreover, the temporal sequence of stimuli and responses differs between the two forms of conditioning. Classical conditioning involves the presentation of the conditioned stimulus prior to the unconditioned stimulus, leading to the learned association, whereas in operant conditioning, the consequence follows the behavior, influencing the likelihood of its recurrence. Additionally, the concept of contingency is central to operant conditioning but plays a less prominent role in classical conditioning. Contingency refers to the predictable relationship between behavior and consequence, highlighting the instrumental nature of operant learning. Understanding these fundamental differences between classical and operant conditioning is vital for comprehending the diverse mechanisms through which organisms learn and adapt to their environment.

Core Concepts - Behavior, Consequence, Contingency

The core concepts of behavior, consequence, and contingency form the cornerstone of operant conditioning theory and practice. Behavior refers to any observable and measurable action or response exhibited by an individual, ranging from simple motor movements to complex cognitive processes. In the context of operant conditioning, behavior is the target for modification through the application of reinforcement or punishment. Consequence, on the other hand, encompasses the outcomes that follow a specific behavior. These consequences can either reinforce or suppress the occurrence of the behavior, thereby shaping the individual's future responses. Understanding the role of consequences in behavior modification is essential for practitioners and researchers alike. Contingency, the third core concept, pertains to the predictive relationship between behavior and its consequences. It delineates the cause-and-effect link between an individual's actions and the ensuing outcomes. By comprehending the contingent nature of behavior-consequence associations, psychologists can effectively design and implement intervention strategies. Furthermore, this insight allows for the systematic analysis and manipulation of contingencies to bring about desired behavioral changes. The interplay among behavior, consequence, and contingency forms the foundation upon which operant conditioning principles are applied in various settings. Real-world applications of these core concepts abound, spanning from clinical interventions for maladaptive behaviors to productivity enhancement in organizational environments. As such, cultivating a nuanced understanding of behavior-consequence relationships and contingencies is paramount for professionals working in fields where behavioral modification and management are central concerns.

Role of Reinforcement in Behavior Modification

Reinforcement, a fundamental concept in operant conditioning, plays a pivotal role in behavior modification. By understanding the mechanisms and applications of reinforcement, psychologists and educators can effectively shape and alter human and animal behavior. Reinforcement encompasses the strategic use of stimuli to increase the likelihood of a specific behavior recurring. Whether positive or negative, reinforcement offers a powerful tool for modifying behavior in diverse settings, ranging from classrooms to clinical interventions.

Positive reinforcement involves the introduction of a rewarding stimulus immediately following a desired behavior, thereby strengthening the likelihood of that behavior being repeated. This positive stimulus could be anything that is perceived as favorable by the individual, such as praise, tangible rewards, or privileges. In contrast, negative reinforcement entails the removal of an aversive stimulus after the performance of a desired behavior, thereby reinforcing the likelihood of that behavior occurring again. Despite the differences between positive and negative reinforcement, both methods demonstrate the potency of reinforcement in shaping behavior.

Behavior modification, a key application of reinforcement, aims to instill new behaviors or eliminate undesired ones through systematic reinforcement strategies. When developing behavior modification plans, professionals carefully select and administer reinforcements tailored to the individual's unique needs and learning profile. This tailored approach ensures that reinforcement aligns with the person's preferences, motivation, and developmental stage, maximizing its effectiveness. Notably, behavioral modification based on reinforcement has been extensively used in various fields, including special education, developmental disabilities, rehabilitation, and organizational behavior management. The process involves identifying target behaviors, designing reinforcement schedules, and continuously monitoring progress to ascertain the effectiveness of the applied reinforcement techniques.

Understanding the complex interplay between reinforcement and behavior fosters the development of evidence-based interventions that promote adaptive behavior change. Moreover, the strategic utilization of reinforcement acknowledges the reciprocal influence of environmental variables and personality traits on behavior. By incorporating reinforcement into behavior modification practices, practitioners can empower individuals to attain meaningful and sustainable behavioral transformations. Hence, the critical role of reinforcement in behavior modification underscores its significance in promoting positive change and fostering growth in individuals across various contexts.

The Influence of Environmental Variables

Environmental variables encompass a broad spectrum of factors that contribute to shaping an individual's actions and responses. These variables include but are not limited to social interactions, physical surroundings, cultural norms, and situational triggers. It is essential to recognize the dynamic and reciprocal relationship between an organism and its environment. The impact of environmental variables lies at the core of operant conditioning principles, as they determine the likelihood of behaviors being repeated or diminished.

In understanding the influence of environmental variables, one must consider the concept of stimulus control. Stimulus control refers to the capacity of specific cues or stimuli in the environment to evoke particular responses from an individual. For instance, in a workplace setting, the sound of a ringing telephone may prompt an employee to answer it promptly, thereby demonstrating the control exerted by the environmental stimulus. Moreover, the consistency and predictability of the environment play a pivotal role in the reinforcement of behaviors. An environment characterized by consistent consequences for certain behaviors reinforces the association between the action and its outcomes.

The social environment significantly impacts operant conditioning. Social reinforcements, such as praise, approval, or criticism, wield substantial influence on an individual's behavior. By altering the social context and interactions, one can effectively shape and modify behaviors through selective reinforcement techniques. Similarly, observational learning, a concept closely related to operant conditioning, is profoundly influenced by environmental variables. Individuals often mimic behaviors observed in their surroundings, further emphasizing the impact of the environment on behavioral acquisition and modification.

Environmental variables also extend to the impact of cultural practices, societal norms, and historical contexts. Cultural variations in reinforcement practices and acceptable behaviors hint at the relationship between environment and behavior. Different cultures may place varying emphasis on certain behaviors and reinforcement mechanisms, thereby illustrating the contextual nature of operant conditioning processes.

Observational Examples of Operant Conditioning in Nature

Operant conditioning can be observed throughout the natural world, providing insightful illustrations of how organisms adapt their behaviors based on consequences. One prominent example is seen in the foraging behaviors of animals such as birds and primates. When a bird learns that pecking at a specific colored object on a tree results in receiving food, this represents a classic case of operant conditioning. Through repeated experiences, the bird comes to associate the act of pecking with obtaining sustenance, thereby reinforcing this behavior.

Similarly, among primates, the utilization of tools for obtaining food showcases operant conditioning principles. For instance, when a chimpanzee learns to use a stick to extract insects from a crevice, the successful extraction of food serves as a positive consequence, reinforcing the behavior of using the stick as a tool. Over time, this behavior becomes more frequent and refined as the primate learns through the reinforcing outcomes.

Another striking instance of operant conditioning in nature is evident in the predatory behaviors of carnivorous species. Predators that engage in stalking and hunting activities rely on operant conditioning to refine their techniques and strategies for capturing prey. The success or failure of a hunting attempt acts as a potent reinforcer, shaping subsequent predatory behaviors. For instance, a lion that successfully captures its prey is likely to repeat the same approach in the future, associating it with a positive outcome. Conversely, if a hunting tactic fails to secure a meal, the predator may modify its approach in subsequent attempts, demonstrating the influence of operant conditioning on adaptive behaviors in the natural world.

Within the social dynamics of animal groups, operant conditioning plays a pivotal role in the establishment of hierarchies and the regulation of social behavior. Dominance displays among certain species, such as wolves or primates, are often reinforced through operant mechanisms. Individuals that assert dominance successfully may receive preferential access to resources, mating opportunities, or social status, thus reinforcing their dominant behaviors. On the other hand, subordinates may modify their behavior to avoid confrontation or gain favor with dominant individuals, reflecting the impact of operant conditioning on social dynamics within animal communities.

Significance of Operant Conditioning in Behavioral Psychology

One of the primary contributions of operant conditioning to behavioral psychology lies in its emphasis on observable behaviors and their consequences. Unlike some other psychological theories that focus primarily on internal cognitive processes, operant conditioning directs attention to the measurable outcomes of behavior. This tangible and empirical approach has facilitated the development of evidence-based interventions and treatment strategies in various clinical settings.

Operant conditioning has been instrumental in elucidating the complex relationship between behavior and environmental stimuli. By recognizing the role of external factors in shaping behavior, psychologists can design targeted interventions to modify and reinforce adaptive behaviors while minimizing maladaptive responses. This has widespread applications in clinical psychology, education, and organizational behavior management.

The principles of operant conditioning have provided a solid foundation for developing effective behavioral therapies. Techniques such as applied behavior analysis (ABA) have demonstrated remarkable success in addressing behavioral challenges across diverse populations, including individuals with autism spectrum disorders, developmental disabilities, and psychiatric conditions. The systematic application of operant conditioning principles within behavioral therapies has significantly improved the quality of life for many individuals and fostered advancements in the field of behavioral healthcare.

In addition, the study of operant conditioning has contributed to a deeper understanding of motivation and reinforcement mechanisms, shedding light on the underlying processes that drive and maintain behavior. This knowledge has informed the development of motivational strategies in various fields, such as education, business management, and sports coaching, enhancing performance and cultivating positive behavioral patterns.

Initial Criticisms and Acceptance within the Scientific Community

Operant conditioning, despite its crucial contributions to the field of psychology, faced initial criticisms and skepticism within the scientific community. When this behaviorist approach emerged, it challenged prevailing notions of human behavior and learning. Many psychologists were accustomed to theories centered around innate drives and instincts, and operant conditioning presented a radical departure from these traditional perspectives. Furthermore, some critics dismissed operant conditioning as overly simplistic, arguing that it failed to account for the complexities of human cognition and emotion.

One notable criticism arose from cognitive psychologists who contended that operant conditioning neglected the role of mental processes in shaping behavior. They argued that individuals do not merely respond to external stimuli, but actively process information and make decisions based on their thoughts and beliefs. This debate sparked the enduring 'cognitive revolution' in psychology, which emphasized the importance of internal mental states and greatly impacted the development of psychological theories and research methodologies.

Operant conditioning encountered resistance due to ethical concerns surrounding the use of reinforcement and punishment in behavior modification. Critics questioned the morality of employing these principles to influence human behavior, particularly in educational and clinical settings. The potential misuse and abuse of behavioral techniques also raised apprehensions about the ethical implications of operant conditioning practices.

Notwithstanding these initial criticisms, operant conditioning gradually gained acceptance within the scientific community as empirical evidence accumulated in support of its principles. Behavioral researchers demonstrated the effectiveness of operant conditioning in diverse contexts, ranging from animal training to therapeutic interventions. Through meticulous experimentation and systematic observation, they provided compelling evidence for the predictive power and practical applicability of operant conditioning.

The ongoing refinement of operant conditioning principles and methodologies addressed many of the prior criticisms. Researchers expanded their focus to encompass cognitive elements within the framework of operant conditioning, thus reconciling some of the earlier disputes between behaviorism and cognitive psychology. Additionally, ethical guidelines and standards were established to govern the ethical usage of operant conditioning techniques, alleviating concerns regarding potential harm or exploitation.

Relevance and Contributions to Modern Psychological Practices

In clinical psychology, operant conditioning techniques have been utilized in various therapeutic interventions, particularly in behavior modification and rehabilitation programs. These techniques have been effective in addressing a multitude of behavioral issues, including addiction, phobias, and antisocial behaviors. By systematically applying reinforcement and punishment strategies, clinicians have successfully reshaped maladaptive behaviors and reinforced positive behavioral changes in their patients. Moreover, the principles of operant conditioning have informed evidence-based interventions for individuals with developmental disabilities, providing practical frameworks for skill acquisition and self-management. Within the field of education, operant conditioning has been integral in shaping instructional strategies and classroom management techniques. By understanding the principles of reinforcement and shaping, educators have been able to design effective teaching methodologies, enhance student engagement, and foster a conducive learning environment. Furthermore, operant conditioning concepts have elucidated the effectiveness of behavior management plans in promoting desirable behaviors among students and curbing undesirable conduct. Employers and organizations have also leveraged operant conditioning principles in shaping workplace behaviors and performance. Through the implementation of reward systems and performance-based incentives, companies have sought to motivate employees, reinforce desired work habits, and cultivate a culture of productivity. Additionally, operant conditioning has provided a foundation for understanding consumer behaviors and marketing strategies, allowing businesses to influence consumer choices and preferences. As the field of psychology continues to evolve, the contributions of operant conditioning remain indispensable in elucidating the complexities of human behavior and guiding evidence-based interventions. Further advancements in technology and research methodologies continue to expand the scope of operant conditioning, paving the way for innovative applications in diverse psychological domains.

B. F. SKINNER - HISTORICAL CONTEXT & BACKGROUND

Early Influences and Educational Background

Burrhus Frederic Skinner, often known as B.F. Skinner, was influenced by his upbringing and educational experiences in shaping his theoretical approaches within psychology. Born on March 20, 1904, in Susquehanna, Pennsylvania, Skinner grew up in a warm and intellectually stimulating environment that encouraged curiosity and exploration. His parents, William and Grace Skinner, played a pivotal role in fostering his early interest in learning and inquiry. Skinner's formative years were marked by exposure to literature, music, and philosophical discussions, which greatly contributed to the development of his inquisitive mind.

Skinner's educational journey commenced at Hamilton College, where he initially pursued a degree in English literature. However, his academic trajectory took an unexpected turn when he became engrossed in psychology after enrolling in a psychology course with Professor William R. Hamilton. This experience ignited Skinner's passion for understanding human behavior and served as a catalyst for his eventual transition into the field of psychology.

Following his undergraduate studies, Skinner continued to delve into psychology, obtaining a master's degree in 1930 from Harvard University. His time at Harvard exposed him to influential figures such as William James and E.B. Titchener, whose teachings and philosophies significantly influenced Skinner's early conceptualizations of behaviorism.

Skinner's exposure to the works of Ivan Pavlov and John B. Watson during his graduate studies further fueled his interest in behavioral psychology. Their pioneering research paved the way for Skinner's own groundbreaking contributions to the field, providing a solid foundation for his future endeavors in experimental analysis of behavior.

It is evident that Skinner's formative years and educational experiences laid the groundwork for his revolutionary theories in psychology. The interdisciplinary nature of his upbringing and academic pursuits not only broadened his intellectual horizons but also instilled in him a deep-seated appreciation for empirical inquiry and scientific rigor. These early influences set the stage for Skinner's remarkable career and the enduring impact of his theoretical frameworks on the field of psychology.

Initial Foray into Psychology

Skinner's initial foray into psychology marked the commencement of what would later become a profoundly influential career in behavioral science. After completing his undergraduate studies at Hamilton College, Skinner ventured into the world of literature, exploring his passion for writing as a newspaper writer and aspiring novelist. This period was pivotal in shaping his unique perspective on human behavior, as he delved into the intricacies of language and human expression. However, it was his enrollment in Harvard University's psychology program that catalyzed his transition into the field of experimental psychology. Under the mentorship of eminent psychologists such as William James and E.B. Holt, Skinner honed his understanding of psychological phenomena and the foundations of behaviorism. His exposure to the pioneering theories of John B Watson instilled in him a fervent zeal for unraveling the complexities of human behavior through empirical observation and experimentation. This period of academic immersion laid the groundwork for Skinner's lifelong dedication to elucidating the fundamental principles of behavior and learning.

Skinner's early forays into experimental psychology were characterized by an unyielding curiosity and tenacity to explore novel avenues of inquiry. Influenced by the scientific rigor championed by his mentors, Skinner embarked on a series of empirical investigations that sought to discern observable patterns in behavior. His engagement with the burgeoning field of animal psychology proved instrumental in shaping his paradigm-shifting contributions to the understanding of operant conditioning. The prodigious insights garnered during this juncture in Skinner's academic journey ultimately fueled his unwavering commitment to revolutionizing the study of behavior and cultivating a comprehensive framework for behavioral analysis.

Unfettered by conventional paradigms, Skinner's early ventures into psychology foreshadowed his unrelenting pursuit of scientific inquiry and empirical rigor. As he delved deeper into the fabric of human behavior, Skinner's inquisitive spirit and penchant for systematic inquiry crystallized, laying a solid foundation for his groundbreaking forays into the fields of behavioral theory and operant conditioning. This phase of formative exploration not only equipped Skinner with a profound appreciation for the pertinence of environmental contingencies in shaping behavior but also infused his scholarly undertakings with an indefatigable resolve to decode the mechanisms underpinning human conduct. Ultimately, it was this formative phase that set the stage for Skinner to emerge as a trailblazing figure in the annals of behavioral psychology.

Development of Behavioral Theories

B. F. Skinner's r exploration into the intricacies of behavior commenced with a desire to create a comprehensive system for understanding and predicting behavior. Through meticulous observations and experiments, Skinner sought to decipher the underlying mechanisms that drive human actions and reactions. This endeavor marked the genesis of his groundbreaking work in behavioral psychology.

Skinner's in-depth analysis of behavior began with the observation of external stimuli and their effects on an organism's responses. His pioneering research unveiled the core principles of classical and operant conditioning, laying the foundation for a profound transformation in psychological thought. By rigorously studying the influence of reinforcements and punishments on behavior, Skinner uncovered fundamental truths about how individuals learn and adapt in their environments.

Central to the development of behavioral theories was Skinner's dedication to empirical evidence and systematic inquiry. He meticulously designed controlled experiments to test and validate his hypotheses, shaping the scientific rigor that underpinned his contributions to psychology. Through these empirical investigations, Skinner elucidated the principles of shaping behaviors through positive and negative reinforcements, fundamentally altering conventional understandings of human behavior.

Skinner's focus on the operant behavior of organisms expanded the horizons of behavioral psychology. His innovative research shed light on the complex interplay between behavior and its consequences, leading to profound insights into the mechanisms governing human and animal behavior. By delineating the dynamics of reinforcement schedules and their impact on behavior, Skinner demonstrated the nature of behavioral conditioning, establishing a paradigm shift in psychological paradigms.

Skinner's development of behavioral theories transcended academia, permeating diverse domains such as education, therapy, and organizational management. His influential concepts provided practical frameworks for shaping behavior, fostering the evolution of effective teaching methods and therapeutic interventions. The widespread applications of Skinner's theories underscored their transformative impact on various facets of human interaction and societal dynamics.

The Emergence of Operant Conditioning Theory

Skinner's work at the Harvard Psychological Laboratories marked a pivotal juncture in the development of psychological theory and experimentation. His foray into investigating the principles of operant conditioning was underpinned by a meticulous approach to observation and data collection. Skinner's meticulous attention to detail and precise experimental techniques led to the emergence of operant conditioning theory, which fundamentally challenged conventional wisdom about human behavior and learning. As he delved deeper into the dynamics of behavioral responses, Skinner postulated that behavior is shaped by its consequences, emphasizing the role of reinforcement and punishment in molding individual actions. This pioneering paradigm shift laid the foundation for a new era of psychological inquiry, elucidating the nuanced interplay between environmental factors and behavioral outcomes. Skinner's groundbreaking research not only bolstered the empirical rigor of psychological inquiry but also offered practical applications across diverse domains, reshaping the landscape of psychology and education. The emergence of operant conditioning theory brought forth a rich tapestry of experimental findings and theoretical constructs, unveiling the intricacies of behavior modification and shaping. Through systematic exploration and rigorous experimentation, Skinner unveiled the underlying mechanisms governing voluntary actions, paving the way for a comprehensive understanding of human and animal behavior. The profound impact of operant conditioning theory transcended academic spheres, permeating into fields such as organizational behavior, clinical therapy, and animal training.

Significant Publications and Works

Throughout his career, B.F. Skinner made groundbreaking contributions to the field of psychology through his significant publications and influential works. His extensive body of work has not only shaped the evolution of behavioral psychology but has also had a profound impact on various other disciplines. One of Skinner's most renowned publications is his seminal book 'The Behavior of Organisms' (1938), wherein he laid the theoretical foundations for operant conditioning. This work revolutionized the understanding of behavior and paved the way for the development of applied behavioral analyses in diverse fields. Subsequently, Skinner published 'Walden Two' (1948), a fictional utopian novel that explored the practical application of behavioral principles in societal organization and governance. The thought-provoking concepts presented in this work sparked widespread discussion about the possibilities of behaviorally engineered societies. Another milestone in Skinner's literary legacy is 'Science and Human Behavior' (1953), which elaborated on the empirical and philosophical underpinnings of behaviorism as a scientific framework. Furthermore, his opus magnum, 'Beyond Freedom and Dignity' (1971), challenged traditional notions of free will and moral responsibility, presenting a controversial perspective on human behavior and society. In addition to these pivotal writings, Skinner authored numerous scholarly articles and essays that delved into topics ranging from operant conditioning mechanisms to the ethical implications of behavioral interventions. Moreover, his inventive contributions extended beyond the field of traditional publications, with the design of experimental apparatus such as the 'Skinner Box' profoundly impacting the methodology of psychological research.

Influence on Contemporary Psychology

B. F. Skinner's influence on contemporary psychology is profound and far-reaching. One of his most significant contributions lies in shaping the behaviorist movement and fostering a deeper understanding of human behavior through empirical observations and systematic analysis. His emphasis on observable behaviors and environmental factors engendered a paradigm shift in psychological inquiry, laying the groundwork for the development of behavior modification techniques and applied behavior analysis. These practical applications have found extensive use in various domains such as education, clinical psychology, and organizational behavior management. Additionally, Skinner's advocacy for determinism in behavior, disavowing the role of introspection and mentalistic explanations, has stimulated ongoing debates about the nature of human agency and the interplay between genetics, environment, and learned behaviors. Furthermore, his work has had a pervasive impact on the study of animal behavior, influencing ethology and comparative psychology. By elucidating the principles of operant conditioning, Skinner established a framework for understanding how organisms learn and adapt to their environment, thus enriching the broader understanding of learning processes. His experimental and theoretical contributions continue to provide fertile ground for contemporary research endeavors, shaping fields such as cognitive psychology, developmental psychology, and behavioral economics. Moreover, Skinner's pioneering work in the design of controlled environments and shaping behavior through reinforcement schedules has informed advancements in experimental methodologies and laboratory settings, transcending the fields of psychology into other disciplines such as neuroscience and human-computer interaction. The enduring legacy of Skinner's scholarship extends beyond academic pursuits and permeates popular culture, whereby concepts such as positive reinforcement and behavior modification have penetrated public discourse and everyday practices, underpinning approaches to parenting, teaching, and organizational management.

Collaborations and Major Research Projects

One of B. F. Skinner's pivotal partnerships was with his colleague and wife, Yvonne Blue Skinner, who played an integral role in supporting and contributing to his groundbreaking work. Together, they conducted extensive research on operant conditioning and its applications, exploring the mechanisms of behavior modification and reinforcement schedules.

Skinner's collaborative endeavors extended beyond academia, as he actively engaged with various scholars, psychologists, and researchers to investigate diverse aspects of human behavior. Notably, his collaboration with leading figures in the field led to the development of innovative techniques and experimental designs that revolutionized the understanding of operant conditioning and its practical implications.

Skinner spearheaded several major research projects that left an indelible mark on the discipline. His pioneering studies delved into topics such as behavioral therapy, animal learning, and the application of operant conditioning principles in real-world settings. These ambitious undertakings not only expanded the breadth of knowledge in behavioral psychology but also laid the groundwork for numerous therapeutic interventions and educational strategies.

In addition to his individual contributions, Skinner's collaboration with prominent institutions and organizations worldwide amplified the impact of his research. His involvement in multidisciplinary initiatives facilitated the integration of behavioral principles into diverse fields, ranging from education and healthcare to organizational management and public policy. This holistic approach underscored Skinner's commitment to advancing the practical and theoretical fields of behavioral science through collective expertise and shared resources.

Awards, Recognitions, and Legacy

Skinner's pioneering work in the field of behavioral psychology has been widely recognized and celebrated, resulting in numerous accolades, awards, and honors throughout his illustrious career. Skinner's most prestigious accolade was the National Medal of Science, which he received from President Lyndon B. Johnson in 1968. This esteemed award highlighted Skinner's significant contributions to the advancement of behavioral science and solidified his position as a prominent figure in the field. In addition to the National Medal of Science, Skinner also received the American Psychological Association (APA) Distinguished Scientific Contribution Award for his groundbreaking research in operant conditioning and behavioral analysis. This recognition further underscored the lasting impact of Skinner's work on psychological science and practice. Furthermore, Skinner's enduring influence is evidenced by the establishment of the B. F. Skinner Foundation, an organization dedicated to preserving and promoting his legacy. The foundation serves as a testament to Skinner's enduring impact and commitment to advancing the understanding of human behavior. Beyond formal accolades and organizations, Skinner's legacy can be seen in the widespread application of his theories in various fields, including education, therapy, and animal training. His innovative techniques and principles have had a profound influence on the development of effective teaching methods, behavior modification strategies, and therapeutic interventions. Although Skinner faced criticisms and controversies during his lifetime, his legacy continues to shape the landscape of modern psychology and remains a cornerstone of behavioral research and practice.

Challenges Faced and Criticisms

Throughout his career, B. F. Skinner encountered numerous challenges and criticisms that shaped the discourse surrounding his work in behavioral psychology. One of the primary challenges Skinner faced was the resistance from traditional psychologists who were skeptical of his radical behaviorist approach, which focused solely on observable behavior and eschewed the study of internal mental processes. This led to significant tension within the academic community and posed obstacles to the widespread acceptance of Skinner's theories. Additionally, some critics raised concerns about the ethical implications of behavior modification techniques advocated by Skinner, particularly in the context of applied settings such as education and therapy. The potential for misuse and coercion in applying operant conditioning methods became a point of contention among scholars and practitioners. Moreover, Skinner's rejection of free will and emphasis on environmental determinants of behavior attracted criticism from humanistic and existential psychologists who espoused the importance of individual agency and personal autonomy. This philosophical divergence sparked debates about the nature of human nature and the implications of deterministic perspectives on human behavior. Another notable challenge faced by Skinner was the difficulty in reconciling his deterministic framework with the complexities of human behavior, including creativity, self-expression, and intrinsic motivation. Critics argued that operant conditioning failed to fully account for these aspects of human experience, thereby limiting its explanatory and predictive power.

FUNDAMENTAL PRINCIPLES AND KEY CONCEPTS

The Definition of Behavior in Operant Conditioning

1. Behavior's Conceptualization in Psychological Frameworks:

Behavior, within the context of operant conditioning, is deeply rooted in various psychological frameworks that seek to conceptualize and understand its dynamics. One such approach is the behaviorist perspective, which emphasizes observable behaviors and their association with external stimuli. This perspective, championed by figures such as B.F. Skinner, focuses on how environmental factors shape behavior through reinforcement and punishment processes. Furthermore, the cognitive-behavioral approach delves into the interplay between thoughts, emotions, and behaviors, highlighting the role of cognitive processes in shaping individual actions. Additionally, the psychodynamic perspective, popularized by Sigmund Freud, delves into the influence of unconscious drives and past experiences on behavior, offering a more introspective lens. Evolutionary psychology contributes by exploring how behaviors may have evolved to confer adaptive advantages to individuals. Such diverse psychological approaches add depth to the understanding of behavior within operant conditioning, providing valuable insights into the multifaceted nature of behavioral dynamics. Moreover, these concepts underscore the importance of considering not only the observable actions but also the underlying mental processes and historical context that influence and define behavior. By integrating these approaches, operant conditioning can be enhanced to account for the complex interplay between biological, cognitive, emotional, and environmental factors in shaping behavior.

2. Historical Perspectives on Behavioral Definition:

The concept of behavior has been a focal point of inquiry across diverse intellectual traditions, ranging from philosophy to psychology. In classical antiquity, the philosophical discourse of human behavior was intertwined with moral and ethical considerations, as evidenced in the works of philosophers such as Plato and Aristotle. The notion of habituation and its influence on behavior found prominence in the writings of these ancient scholars, laying a foundational understanding of behavioral patterns.

With the advent of modern psychology, the conceptualization of behavior underwent pivotal transformations. The introspective methods of structuralism gave way to the experimental rigor of behaviorism, spearheaded by figures like Ivan Pavlov, John B. Watson, and B.F. Skinner. Behaviorists emphasized the objective study of observable behaviors, eschewing internal mental processes and focusing on the environmental stimuli that shape actions. This shift marked a decisive departure from the earlier philosophical and introspective approaches to understanding human conduct.

Throughout the 20th century, the field of psychology witnessed an unprecedented surge in research dedicated to unraveling the intricacies of behavior. Notably, the contributions of behaviorists have elucidated the link between stimulus and response, paving the way for operant conditioning as a fundamental principle in shaping behavior. The systematic exploration of how consequences influence the likelihood of behavior recurring has been instrumental in refining our comprehension of behavioral dynamics.

The historical narrative underscores the interdisciplinary nature of behavioral studies, encompassing fields such as neuroscience, ethology, and cognitive psychology. Researchers have sought to integrate findings from diverse disciplines to construct a comprehensive framework for delineating the multifaceted nature of behavior. This convergence of knowledge streams has enriched the historical trajectory of behavioral definitions, fostering a more nuanced and holistic approach to understanding the complexities of human and animal behavior.

Notwithstanding the paradigm shifts and methodological advancements, historical perspectives remind us of the enduring pursuit to capture the essence of behavior.

3. Core Characteristics of Operant Behavior:

Operant behavior encompasses a diverse set of characteristics that delineate its nature and dynamics. At its core, operant behavior refers to the actions and responses produced by an organism that operate on the surrounding environment and are instrumental in acquiring desired outcomes or reinforcing consequences. One key characteristic of operant behavior is its voluntary nature, which implies that individuals engage in these behaviors deliberately, based on their discretion and assessment of the situational contingencies. Unlike reflexive or involuntary behaviors, operant behaviors are under conscious control and are influenced by the perceived outcomes associated with them. This voluntariness introduces a layer of complexity in understanding behavior as it necessitates an exploration of the cognitive and motivational aspects driving such actions. Additionally, operant behaviors exhibit variability and are not stereotypical in nature. Unlike reflexive behaviors that tend to be relatively fixed and predictable, operant behaviors manifest a degree of flexibility and adaptability shaped by the environmental circumstances and prior learning experiences. This inherent variability reflects the operant nature of these behaviors, emphasizing their sensitivity to contextual cues and reinforcement schedules. Furthermore, operant behaviors are contingent upon the consequences they produce, either increasing or decreasing in frequency based on the nature of the outcome. This contingent relationship between behavior and consequence forms the basis of operant conditioning and underscores the modifiability of behavior through appropriate manipulation of reinforcement and punishment. Another pivotal characteristic of operant behavior is its susceptibility to shaping and modification through systematic interventions, highlighting its malleable nature in response to external influences.

4. Involuntary and Volitional Behaviors:

Involuntary behaviors are those that occur without conscious control or intention, often as a result of reflexes or automatic responses to stimuli in the environment. Examples of involuntary behaviors include reflexive actions like blinking, sneezing, or flinching in response to sudden stimuli. These behaviors are not subject to the same operant principles as volitional behaviors. On the other hand, volitional behaviors are purposeful actions initiated consciously and with intent. These behaviors are under the control of the individual and are influenced by their goals, motivations, and environmental cues. Volitional behaviors often involve decision-making processes and can be shaped and modified through operant conditioning techniques. Understanding the distinction between these two types of behaviors is essential for designing effective behavioral interventions and comprehending the complexities of human and animal behavior. It is also important to recognize that some behaviors may exhibit elements of both involuntariness and volition, further highlighting the nature of behavior and the need for nuanced analyses. Moreover, recognizing and categorizing behaviors based on their voluntariness can aid in identifying appropriate intervention strategies and understanding the underlying mechanisms driving behavioral responses. This differentiation also underscores the multifaceted nature of operant conditioning, as it addresses not only external manifestations of behavior but also the internal cognitive processes and motivational factors that influence volitional behaviors. As such, an investigation into the differential impact of reinforcement and punishment on these distinct categories of behavior can offer valuable insights into how environmental contingencies interact with cognitive and motivational variables to shape behavioral repertoires. Overall, understanding the nuances of involuntary and volitional behaviors is fundamental to the comprehensive study of operant conditioning and provides a rich foundation for promoting meaningful behavioral change and improving outcomes in various domains, including education, clinical psychology, and organizational management.

5. Behavioral Repertoires - Scope and Limitations:

The concept of behavioral repertoires encompasses the range of behaviors that an individual or organism is capable of exhibiting in response to various stimuli and environmental cues. Understanding the scope and limitations of behavioral repertoires is crucial in the context of operant conditioning as it directly influences the potential for behavior modification and learning. From a theoretical standpoint, behavioral repertoires reflect the behavioral diversity of individuals, encompassing both innate and learned behaviors. This diversity is influenced by genetic predispositions, early experiences, and ongoing environmental interactions. It is essential to recognize that behavioral repertoires are not static entities but rather dynamic and subject to change over time. While this adaptability allows for flexibility in responding to new challenges and environments, it also poses certain limitations. One such limitation is the potential narrowness or inflexibility of an individual's repertoire, which may hinder their ability to adapt to novel situations or acquire new behaviors. Furthermore, the existence of maladaptive or dysfunctional behaviors within an individual's repertoire can impede their overall functioning and well-being. In the context of operant conditioning, the scope of behavioral repertoires determines the range of behaviors available for reinforcement or modification. This has implications for shaping desired behaviors and extinguishing unwanted ones. Understanding the limitations of behavioral repertoires is essential for identifying potential barriers to behavior change and developing targeted intervention strategies. Moreover, recognizing the influence of situational factors, such as stressors or environmental constraints, on the expression of specific behaviors is integral to comprehending the boundaries of behavioral repertoires. By acknowledging these limitations, practitioners and researchers can tailor behavioral interventions to effectively address individual needs and promote adaptive behavioral patterns. The exploration of behavioral repertoires extends beyond the individual level to encompass species-specific and cultural variations in behavior. This broader perspective acknowledges the interplay between biological and environmental factors in shaping behavioral repertoires across diverse contexts.

6. Observable and Measurable Criteria for Defining Behavior:

When defining behavior in the context of operant conditioning, it is imperative to establish observable and measurable criteria that can be consistently applied across various settings. Observable criteria refer to the actions, reactions, or responses that are perceptible to an external observer, while measurable criteria entail quantifiable aspects of behavior such as frequency, duration, and intensity. These criteria serve as the foundation for operationalizing behavior, allowing researchers and practitioners to accurately describe, analyze, and modify behavioral patterns. By employing observable and measurable criteria, the ambiguity often associated with subjective interpretations of behavior is mitigated, contributing to the systematic study and application of operant conditioning principles. Central to the process of defining behavior is the comprehensive identification of specific actions or responses pertinent to the individual or subject under examination. This involves the precise delineation of behavioral categories, including both overt behaviors that are directly observable and covert behaviors that may necessitate indirect measurement techniques. Additionally, determining the appropriate time frame and context within which behavior will be assessed is crucial for establishing a reliable and comprehensive behavioral definition. Moreover, discerning the antecedents and consequences that precede and follow the behavior of interest further enhances the operationalization process, encompassing a holistic understanding of behavioral dynamics. As operant conditioning emphasizes the influence of environmental contingencies on behavior, elucidating the functional relationship between stimuli, responses, and reinforcers/punishers becomes integral to the formulation of observable and measurable criteria. In practice, various instruments and methodologies, such as behavior checklists, direct observation, ecological momentary assessment, and psychophysiological measures, can be leveraged to capture behavioral data in a valid and reliable manner. The development of standardized protocols for recording and interpreting behavioral observations helps ensure consistency and objectivity in the assessment process. It is important to acknowledge that the establishment of observable and measurable criteria may encounter challenges when dealing with complex or abstract behaviors, necessitating innovative approaches and interdisciplinary collaboration. Furthermore, considerations related to inter-rater reliability, validity, and ethical implications underscore the need for rigor and diligence in defining behavior within the framework of operant conditioning.

7. Behavior as a Function of its Consequences:

Behavior as a Function of its Consequences elucidates how an organism's actions are shaped and maintained by the environmental outcomes. The theory posits that behavior is functionally related to its consequences, which can be either reinforcing or punishing. Reinforcement increases the likelihood of a behavior recurring, while punishment decreases its occurrence. This principle is rooted in the influential work of B.F. Skinner, who emphasized the central role of consequences in behavioral regulation and modification. At the heart of this concept lies the notion that organisms learn through the outcomes of their actions, thereby adjusting their future behavioral responses. By examining the nature of these consequences, it becomes evident that they wield significant influence over the dynamics of behavior. Further delving into this principle reveals the dichotomy of positive and negative reinforcement, wherein positive reinforcement involves the presentation of a desirable stimulus following a behavior, thus strengthening it, while negative reinforcement entails the removal of an aversive stimulus, also bolstering the likelihood of the behavior reoccurring. Similarly, the mechanisms of punishment entail presenting an undesirable consequence (positive punishment) or removing a favorable stimulus (negative punishment), thereby diminishing the probability of the behavior occurring again. Such dynamic interactions between behavior and its consequences underscore the intricacies of behavioral dynamics. Moreover, this concept's applicability extends beyond individual behavior to encompass social and organizational settings. Understanding how consequences influence behavior enables the design of effective strategies for shaping desired behaviors and curbing maladaptive ones.

8. Notable Theoretical Models of Behavioral Dynamics:

Behavioral dynamics are a complex interplay of numerous factors, and theoretical models provide a framework for understanding and predicting behavioral patterns. One notable theoretical model is the Social Learning Theory proposed by Albert Bandura, which emphasizes the role of observation and imitation in shaping behavior. This model posits that individuals learn from observing others and that behaviors are often acquired through modeling. Bandura's concept of reciprocal determinism, which highlights the influence of personal factors, behavior, and the environment on each other, serves as a foundational aspect of this theory. The Social Learning Theory has significant implications for understanding how individuals acquire new behaviors and how these behaviors are reinforced or extinguished based on observed consequences. Another prominent theoretical model is the Cognitive-Behavioral Theory, which integrates cognitive processes with behavioral principles to explain human behavior. This model emphasizes the role of cognitive appraisal, self-regulation, and belief systems in influencing behavioral patterns. The Cognitive-Behavioral Theory also highlights the significance of environmental reinforcements and punishments in shaping behavior. Furthermore, the Theory of Planned Behavior, developed by Icek Ajzen, focuses on the influence of attitudes, subjective norms, and perceived behavioral control in determining behavioral intentions. This model asserts that an individual's intention to perform a behavior is a strong predictor of actual behavioral performance. Understanding these notable theoretical models offers valuable insights into the multifaceted nature of behavioral dynamics and provides a basis for designing effective interventions and strategies for behavior modification.

9. Integration of Biological Factors in Behavioral Definitions:

The study of behavioral definitions within operant conditioning necessarily involves the incorporation of biological factors to comprehensively understand the complexities of behavior. Biological underpinnings play a crucial role in shaping and influencing behavior, and their integration into behavioral definitions can provide valuable insights into the mechanisms governing operant conditioning.

Neurobiological processes form the foundational basis for understanding behavioral definitions within the framework of operant conditioning. The interplay between neurotransmitters, neural circuits, and brain structures significantly influences an individual's behavioral repertoire. For instance, the dopamine system has been linked to reinforcement processes, highlighting the neurobiological underpinnings of behavioral responses to reinforcing stimuli. Understanding the neural substrates of behavior is essential for developing nuanced definitions that encompass both the psychological and biological dimensions of operant conditioning.

Genetic predispositions contribute to the individual differences observed in behavioral responses, thereby necessitating their incorporation into behavioral definitions. Research in behavioral genetics has elucidated the heritability of certain behavioral traits, emphasizing the need to consider genetic influences when defining and analyzing behavior within operant conditioning paradigms. By integrating genetic factors into behavioral definitions, researchers and practitioners can gain a more comprehensive understanding of the variability in individual responses to operant stimuli, thereby refining behavioral definitions and interventions.

In addition to neurobiological and genetic influences, the role of physiological mechanisms in shaping behavioral responses must be considered in behavioral definitions. Factors such as hormonal fluctuations, metabolic processes, and autonomic nervous system activity can profoundly impact an individual's behavioral tendencies. Accounting for these physiological factors in behavioral definitions ensures a holistic approach to understanding behavior, encompassing the interplay between biological, psychological, and environmental determinants.

10. Challenges and Debates in Defining Operant Behavior:

One of the primary challenges in defining operant behavior arises from the inherent subjectivity involved in identifying and categorizing behaviors within the framework of operant conditioning. Unlike physiological processes that can be objectively measured, behaviors are often influenced by individual perceptions, cultural norms, and contextual factors, making it difficult to arrive at universally applicable definitions. This subjectivity gives rise to ongoing debates regarding the criteria for defining and classifying operant behaviors.

Another significant challenge revolves around the contextual nature of behavior and the role of situational factors in shaping and determining behavioral responses. The dynamic interaction between an organism and its environment complicates the process of isolating and defining specific behaviors, as behaviors may manifest differently in varied contexts. Moreover, the influence of cultural, social, and environmental variables adds layers of complexity to the task of delineating operant behaviors, leading to disagreements and discussions regarding the generalizability of defined behaviors across diverse settings.

The concept of intentionality and volition in operant behaviors has been a subject of debate. While some scholars emphasize the volitional aspect of operant behaviors, attributing them to conscious goal-directed actions, others argue that many behaviors occur involuntarily or reflexively, blurring the lines between operant and respondent behaviors. This debate has implications for the precise demarcation of operant behaviors and the criteria used to differentiate them from other types of behavioral responses.

Additionally, the ethical considerations surrounding the definition of operant behavior have sparked deliberations within the field. As researchers strive to clarify and categorize behaviors for experimental and therapeutic purposes, questions arise about the potential impact of these definitions on individuals' autonomy, dignity, and rights. Ethical debates center on issues such as the labelling and pathologizing of behaviors, especially in the context of mental health and educational interventions, prompting critical reflections on the societal implications of defining operant behaviors.

The Role of the Environment in Shaping Behavior

1. Environmental Influences on Behavioral Patterns:

The interaction between organisms and their environment plays a pivotal role in shaping and modifying behavior. Environmental influences encompass a wide array of factors, including physical surroundings, social interactions, cultural norms, and situational contexts. This complex interplay between individuals and their environment contributes significantly to the development and expression of behavioral patterns. Moreover, environmental stimuli can evoke both overt and covert responses in individuals, thereby shaping their behavioral repertoire. By analyzing the reciprocal relationship between organisms and their surroundings, researchers gain insight into the processes through which environmental variables impact behavioral outcomes. The nuances of environmental influences on behavior are further underscored by their role in mediating reinforcement schedules and response contingencies. These environmental variables, when carefully manipulated, can serve as potent tools for instigating and maintaining specific behavioral responses. Additionally, adaptive behavior to environmental changes highlights the dynamic nature of this relationship, as individuals continually adjust their behavioral strategies in response to varying environmental demands. Stimulus control, a critical concept in behavioral analysis, elucidates how environmental cues regulate and modulate behavioral responses, underscoring the profound influence of the environment on shaping behavior. Crucially, the design of environments can be tailored to elicit desired behavioral outcomes, as evidenced by successful applications of environmental engineering in diverse settings. Case studies that document the impact of environmental variables on behavior provide valuable empirical evidence supporting the pivotal role of the environment in shaping behavioral patterns.

2. The Interaction between Organisms and Their Environment:

The interaction between organisms and their environment is at the heart of behavioral analysis in operant conditioning. This interaction involves a complex interplay between an organism's behavior and the surrounding environment, encompassing physical, social, and situational factors. Organisms respond to their environment through various behavioral patterns, which are influenced by stimuli, reinforcement, and the broader context in which they exist. Understanding this interaction provides valuable insights into how behavior is shaped and modified.

At the core of this interaction is the concept of reciprocal determinism, proposed by psychologist Albert Bandura. Reciprocal determinism suggests that behavior, environmental factors, and personal characteristics continually influence each other. This means that individuals not only respond to environmental stimuli but also actively shape and modify their environment through their actions, creating a dynamic relationship between organism and environment. In turn, the environment provides feedback and consequences that further influence the individual's behavior, leading to a continuous cycle of interaction.

The concept of operant behavior emphasizes that an organism's behavior operates on its environment, producing consequences that can either reinforce or suppress the behavior. Additionally, this understanding allows us to manipulate environmental conditions to facilitate desired behavioral outcomes.

An organism's environment encompasses both the physical setting and the social context in which it operates. Environmental stimuli, such as rewards and punishments, play a pivotal role in shaping an organism's behavior. Moreover, the social environment, including interactions with conspecifics and caregivers, influences an organism's learning and behavioral development. It is therefore essential to consider the multifaceted nature of an organism's environment when analyzing behavioral patterns.

The interaction between organisms and their environment is not limited to immediate experiences. The broader ecological context, encompassing cultural, societal, and historical factors, also exerts a profound influence on behavioral patterns. This emphasizes the importance of considering the macro-level environmental influences that contribute to shaping behavior, providing a holistic perspective on the interaction between organisms and their surroundings.

3. The Importance of Context in Behavioral Analysis:

In behavioral analysis, the significance of context cannot be overstated, as it encompasses the environmental, social, and situational factors that influence an individual's actions and reactions. The immediate surroundings and situational cues interplay with an individual's psychological and physiological state, creating a unique context for every behavior observed. Understanding the influence of context allows researchers and practitioners to gain insight into the antecedents and consequences that shape behavior. Furthermore, recognizing the multi-faceted nature of context sheds light on how different environments can elicit varied responses from individuals. A comprehensive examination of context provides a deeper understanding of why certain behaviors manifest in specific situations. Moreover, contextual analysis enables the identification of triggers and disturbances within an environment that may contribute to maladaptive or undesirable behaviors. It also highlights the dynamic nature of behavior, underscoring the impact of changes in context on behavioral adjustments. By scrutinizing the contextual factors at play, we can identify patterns and trends, facilitating targeted interventions for behavioral modification.

4. Environmental Stimuli:

Environmental stimuli play a crucial role in shaping behavior and influencing behavioral responses. These stimuli can be broadly categorized into various types, each exerting specific effects on individuals within their environment. One key type of environmental stimuli is sensory stimuli, which includes visual, auditory, olfactory, tactile, and gustatory cues. Visual stimuli, for instance, encompass the myriad of images and movements that individuals perceive in their surroundings, while auditory stimuli consist of the diverse sounds and tones that individuals hear. Olfactory stimuli pertain to the countless scents and odors present in the environment, and tactile stimuli involve the sense of touch experienced through physical contact. Finally, gustatory stimuli are related to the tastes and flavors encountered through consumption. Each of these sensory stimuli has the potential to elicit distinct behavioral reactions and shape individuals' responses to their surroundings. Another type of environmental stimulus is social stimuli, which encompasses interactions with other individuals and social cues present in the environment. The presence of peers, leaders, or authoritative figures can significantly impact behavioral patterns, as can non-verbal cues such as body language, facial expressions, and gestures. Moreover, cultural and societal norms also act as influential social stimuli, guiding individuals' behaviors and shaping their responses. In addition to sensory and social stimuli, environmental factors such as temperature, lighting, spatial layout, and even geographical settings constitute environmental stimuli that can affect behavior. For example, research has shown that variations in ambient temperature can impact individuals' moods and activity levels, thus influencing their behavior. Similarly, the presence or absence of natural light can influence circadian rhythms and thereby affect behavioral patterns. Furthermore, spatial layouts and configurations can evoke varied responses from individuals, affecting their movement and interaction patterns. Additionally, geographical settings, such as urban or rural environments, can introduce different environmental stimuli that shape individuals' behavior. Understanding the diverse types of environmental stimuli and their effects is essential for comprehending the dynamics of behavior and the interplay between individuals and their surroundings.

5. Role of Reinforcement Schedules in Environmental Settings:

By understanding and effectively utilizing reinforcement schedules, individuals can influence and modify behavior to achieve desired outcomes. There are several types of reinforcement schedules, each with its distinct impact on behavioral responses. The fixed ratio schedule, for instance, provides reinforcement after a specific number of responses. This can lead to high rates of behavior, as individuals strive to meet the required response count to obtain the reinforcement. On the other hand, the variable ratio schedule delivers reinforcement after an unpredictable number of responses, resulting in persistent and resistant behavior. Understanding these schedules allows for tailored intervention strategies in various environmental contexts.

In environmental settings, the application of reinforcement schedules is often instrumental in promoting and maintaining adaptive behavior. By implementing consistent reinforcement for desirable behaviors, individuals are more likely to exhibit and uphold these behaviors over time. Furthermore, the strategic use of intermittent reinforcement schedules can help prevent extinction of desirable behaviors by intermittently reinforcing them, thus ensuring their continued occurrence despite fluctuating environmental conditions. This aligns with the concept of operant conditioning, wherein reinforcement serves as a mechanism for increasing the likelihood of a specific behavior recurring.

Reinforcement schedules can also be utilized to shape new behaviors within environmental settings. Through the careful establishment of reinforcement contingencies, individuals can prompt the development of novel behaviors that align with desired outcomes. Whether it involves the introduction of positive reinforcement to encourage the adoption of beneficial habits or the implementation of negative reinforcement to mitigate undesirable behaviors, the judicious application of reinforcement schedules holds immense potential for behavior modification within diverse environmental contexts.

It is important to note that the timing and predictability of reinforcement delivery significantly impact behavioral responses within environmental settings. Consistent reinforcement following desirable behaviors tends to yield robust and sustained behavioral patterns. Conversely, erratic or unreliable reinforcement may lead to inconsistent behavioral responses and hinder the desired outcomes. Therefore, understanding the nuances of reinforcement schedules and their implications within environmental settings is pivotal in orchestrating and fostering meaningful behavioral changes.

6. Adaptive Behavior to Environmental Changes:

In the study of operant conditioning, one of the fundamental concepts is the ability of organisms to adapt their behavior in response to changes in the environment. This adaptive behavior is a critical aspect of understanding how individuals learn and modify their actions to achieve favorable outcomes. When confronted with modifications in the environment, organisms display a remarkable capacity for adaptation, often driven by the consequences of their behavior. Adaptive behavior is evident in various aspects of life, from simple everyday activities to complex problem-solving scenarios. The process of adaptability involves a dynamic interplay between the organism's responses and the environmental contingencies that shape those responses.

Understanding how organisms exhibit adaptive behavior to new environmental circumstances is crucial for comprehending the broader implications of operant conditioning. Whether in natural habitats or controlled settings, organisms demonstrate an inherent ability to adjust their behavior according to changing environmental conditions. From foraging strategies in animals to workplace dynamics in human society, the concept of adaptive behavior underscores the pervasive influence of environmental changes on behavioral responses.

The phenomenon of adaptive behavior also highlights the relationship between learning and environmental influences. Organisms continuously assess the impact of their actions within the context of the environment, leading to adjustments in behavior to optimize outcomes. This responsiveness to environmental changes reflects the evolutionary advantage of adaptive behavior, enabling survival and success in diverse ecological niches.

The study of adaptive behavior provides valuable insights into the malleability and resilience of behavioral patterns in the face of environmental variability. By investigating the adaptive responses of organisms to novel stimuli and challenges, researchers gain a deeper understanding of the mechanisms underlying behavioral flexibility and cognitive processes. The analysis of adaptive behavior offers a window into the sophisticated ways in which organisms perceive, interpret, and react to environmental stimuli, shedding light on the workings of behavior-environment interactions.

7. The Concept of Stimulus Control:

In the field of operant conditioning, environmental stimuli has a pivotal role in determining and shaping behavioral responses. This phenomenon pertains to the process through which specific cues or signals influence and regulate the occurrence of a particular behavior. In essence, it delves into the discrimination and generalization of stimuli, elucidating how organisms learn to differentiate between various environmental cues and subsequently exhibit targeted behaviors in response. The interplay between discriminative stimuli, behavioral responses, and reinforcement mechanisms underscores the significance of stimulus control in understanding behavioral dynamics.

Central to this notion is the concept of discriminative stimuli, which refers to the specific cues or signals that evoke a particular response from an organism by signaling the availability of reinforcement. These stimuli essentially set the occasion for the likelihood of a certain behavior occurring, thereby exerting a profound influence on the individual's actions. Through the process of discrimination learning, individuals acquire the ability to distinguish between different stimuli and subsequently modify their behavioral repertoire based on the presence or absence of these stimuli. Moreover, the concept of generalization comes into play, wherein similar stimuli evoke comparable responses due to their resemblance to the original discriminative stimulus, thus showcasing the adaptive nature of behavioral conditioning.

By comprehensively exploring the parameters of stimulus control, we get a deeper understanding of how environmental cues shape behavior and facilitate the acquisition of targeted responses. Additionally, this insight holds significant implications in numerous domains such as education, clinical psychology, and organizational behavior, where deliberate manipulation of environmental stimuli can engender desired behavioral outcomes. Furthermore, the concept of stimulus control extends beyond basic conditioning paradigms, encompassing complex cognitive processes and social interactions, thereby underscoring its multifaceted influence on human behavior.

8. Environmental Design for Desired Behavioral Outcomes:

When considering the design of environments to elicit specific behavioral outcomes, a careful understanding of the principles of operant conditioning is essential. Environmental design for desired behavioral outcomes involves the deliberate arrangement and manipulation of environmental stimuli to promote and reinforce targeted behaviors. It encompasses the intentional structuring of physical surroundings, social settings, and contextual factors to encourage, maintain, or modify behaviors in line with predetermined objectives. This strategic alignment of environmental elements with behavioral goals can yield significant impact and facilitate positive change.

A fundamental aspect of environmental design revolves around the concept of reinforcement. By strategically placing reinforcements within an environment, whether they are tangible rewards, social approval, or other forms of positive reinforcement, individuals are encouraged to exhibit desired behaviors. The spatial arrangement and accessibility of these reinforcing elements can significantly influence the frequency and likelihood of particular behaviors occurring. Likewise, the judicious application of negative reinforcement through the removal of aversive stimuli can also contribute to shaping desired behavioral patterns.

The layout and organization of the environment play a crucial role in guiding behavior. Consider the impact of an educational setting designed to minimize distractions and enhance focus, thereby promoting attentive learning behaviors. Similarly, workplaces structured to facilitate collaboration and communication can foster cooperative and productive work behaviors among employees. These examples underscore the profound influence of environmental design on behavioral outcomes.

Another critical consideration in environmental design pertains to the concept of stimulus generalization and discrimination. Careful attention to the consistency and specificity of environmental cues can influence the extent to which certain behaviors are exhibited. Employing discriminative stimuli to signal when particular behaviors will be reinforced helps individuals distinguish between appropriate and inappropriate responses in varying environmental contexts. This differential reinforcement based on situational cues fosters the development of discriminative operant behaviors while minimizing the occurrence of undesired actions.

Practical applications of environmental design for desired behavioral outcomes extend across diverse domains, including education, clinical interventions, organizational management, and community planning. In educational settings, environmental modifications geared towards enhancing students' engagement, motivation, and learning retention have shown promising results. Within clinical contexts, the deliberate structuring of therapeutic environments can facilitate the acquisition of adaptive behaviors and skills among individuals with diverse needs. Moreover, in organizational management, optimizing the work environment to cultivate desirable work ethic, teamwork, and performance has been linked to improved productivity and job satisfaction.

9. Current Research on Environmental Contributions to Behavior:

Recent studies have significantly advanced our understanding of the relationship between environmental factors and behavioral responses. Cutting-edge research has delved into various aspects, shedding light on how different environments can elicit distinct behaviors in individuals across species and settings. One compelling area of investigation lies in the impact of urban environments on human behavior. Urban psychology research has uncovered the profound influence of city landscapes and structures on human cognition, emotion, and social interactions. Moreover, advancements in technology have allowed for the mapping and analysis of environmental variables, providing a deeper comprehension of how urban design affects human behaviors, from stress levels to decision-making processes.

Current research has expanded beyond human-focused studies to encompass animal behavior in response to environmental stimuli. Scientists are exploring how different habitats, such as natural versus urban landscapes, affect the behavior and survival strategies of various species. By studying the impact of environmental alterations due to human activities, researchers strive to identify measures that could mitigate negative effects and preserve biodiversity. Additionally, investigations into the behavioral consequences of climate change and habitat destruction have garnered attention, driving efforts to comprehend and address the long-term implications for ecosystems and the species within them.

Another noteworthy area of focus in contemporary research involves the role of built environments in shaping organizational and workplace behaviors. Scholars in organizational psychology examine how physical workspaces, such as office layouts and design, influence employee productivity, collaboration, and well-being. This line of inquiry aims to optimize work environments by identifying architectural and design elements that support desired behaviors and enhance overall organizational performance. Moreover, research on environmental psychology in educational settings explores the impacts of school design, classroom layout, and outdoor spaces on student engagement, learning outcomes, and behavior management, offering valuable insights for educational institutions seeking to create conducive learning environments and design solutions to promote positive outcomes at individual, societal, and ecological levels.

Classical vs. Operant Conditioning

1. Introduction to Conditioning Paradigms:

Conditioning paradigms form the cornerstone of behavioral theories and have significantly shaped our understanding of human and animal behavior. These paradigms serve as frameworks for comprehending how learning occurs, and how individuals or organisms adapt their behavior based on experience and environmental stimuli. The historical evolution of conditioning paradigms is intertwined with the development of psychological theories, offering pivotal insights into the mechanisms that underpin behavioral modification. Examining the historical perspective and foundations of conditioning paradigms provides an in-depth exploration of how these theories have evolved over time, leading to paradigm-shifting discoveries and influential theoretical frameworks. From the early experiments of Ivan Pavlov in classical conditioning to the pioneering work of B.F. Skinner in operant conditioning, the lineage of conditioning paradigms reflects a profound shift in our comprehension of behavior and learning processes. Understanding the historical context also allows us to appreciate the diverse philosophical and empirical underpinnings that have contributed to the development of modern behavioral theories. Moreover, delving into the historical foundations offers valuable insights into the influential figures and seminal experiments that have shaped the discourse surrounding conditioning paradigms. By exploring the evolution of conditioning paradigms, we can gain a deeper appreciation for the intricacies of behaviorism and the enduring impact of these fundamental principles on the field of psychology and related disciplines. This historical journey not only elucidates the evolution of conditioning paradigms but also underscores their enduring relevance in contemporary research and practical applications.

2. Historical Perspective and Foundations:

At the turn of the 20th century, Ivan Pavlov's groundbreaking experiments with dogs revealed the principles of classical conditioning, laying the groundwork for understanding how organisms form associations between environmental stimuli and natural responses. These findings not only revolutionized the field of psychology but also set the stage for further exploration into the mechanisms of learning and behavior.

Building upon Pavlov's work, John Watson expanded the paradigm of conditioning by introducing the concept of behaviorism, emphasizing the importance of observable behaviors and rejecting the focus on internal mental processes. By proposing that all behavior could be explained through conditioning, Watson's ideas laid the foundation for the development of operant conditioning and shaped the trajectory of psychological research for decades to come. Moreover, the historical context surrounding the emergence of these paradigms reflects the broader intellectual currents of the time, including a shift towards empirical observation and experimentation, which deeply influenced the direction of psychology as a scientific discipline.

As the field continued to evolve, the work of B.F. Skinner solidified the principles of operant conditioning, exploring the role of reinforcement and punishment in shaping behavior. Skinner's pioneering studies not only provided empirical evidence for the operant conditioning framework but also offered practical applications in fields such as education and clinical therapy. The historical accounts of these prominent figures underscore the progression of conditioning paradigms from theoretical speculation to empirical validation, signifying a transformative era in the history of psychology.

3. Fundamental Principles of Classical Conditioning:

Classical conditioning is attributed to the groundbreaking work of Ivan Pavlov. It involves the association of an unconditioned stimulus with a neutral stimulus to evoke a conditioned response. One of the key principles underlying classical conditioning is the concept of acquisition, wherein the neutral stimulus becomes a conditioned stimulus through repeated pairing with the unconditioned stimulus. Through this process, the organism begins to exhibit a conditioned response to the previously neutral stimulus, demonstrating the acquisition of the learned association.

The phenomenon of extinction plays a pivotal role in classical conditioning. Extinction occurs when the conditioned response diminishes or disappears as a result of the unconditioned stimulus no longer being presented following the conditioned stimulus. This process highlights the importance of continued reinforcement in maintaining conditioned responses. Additionally, spontaneous recovery, observed after a period of rest following extinction, underscores the persistence of the acquired associations, despite temporary setbacks.

Generalization and discrimination are essential concepts in classical conditioning. Generalization refers to the tendency of a previously acquired conditioned response to be elicited not only by the original conditioned stimulus but also by similar stimuli. On the other hand, discrimination involves the ability to differentiate between similar stimuli and respond selectively to the specific conditioned stimulus. Understanding these phenomena provides valuable insights into the nuances of learned behaviors and their applicability in various contexts.

The predictability and timing of stimuli constitute crucial elements in classical conditioning. The contingency between the conditioned and unconditioned stimuli influences the strength and predictability of the resulting conditioned responses. Moreover, the temporal relationship between the stimuli, particularly the precise timing of their presentation, significantly impacts the effectiveness of associative learning. Such considerations are fundamental in elucidating the mechanisms governing classical conditioning and its practical implications.

4. Behavioral Acquisition - Classical vs. Operant Approaches:

Classical conditioning elucidates the association between two stimuli, where an initially neutral stimulus becomes capable of eliciting a response through its pairing with another stimulus that naturally evokes the response. This conditioned response signifies the acquired, learned behavior, exemplifying the pivotal role of involuntary reflexes in this paradigm. On the contrary, operant conditioning centers on the modification of voluntary behaviors through consequences, witnessed in the context of reinforcement or punishment. The fundamental disparity lies in the nature of the elicited response; classical conditioning generates reflexive responses, while operant conditioning fosters deliberate, purposeful actions driven by their outcomes.

Comparatively, classical conditioning predominantly focuses on the development of respondent behavior, characterized by automatic, involuntary reactions, whereas operant conditioning predominantly targets operant behavior, which encompasses intentional actions influenced by their consequences. Moreover, the process of acquisition in classical conditioning entails the establishment of an association between the conditioned and unconditioned stimuli, leading to the eventual transfer of response from the unconditioned to the conditioned stimulus. Contrarily, in operant conditioning, acquisition transpires as the subject associates their behavioral responses with reinforcing or punishing stimuli, thereby exhibiting a compelling influence on future occurrences of the behavior.

It is pertinent to recognize that the distinctions between these acquisition processes extend beyond the nature of learned responses to encompass the foundational learning principles that govern each paradigm. Classical conditioning embodies the significance of contiguity, emphasizing the temporal proximity between the conditioned and unconditioned stimuli, fostering a robust associative bond. In contrast, operant conditioning pivots around the principle of reinforcement, entailing the amplification or diminution of behaviors based on their outcomes, thereby shaping the future likelihood of their occurrence.

The temporal characteristics of the conditioned stimuli markedly differ across the paradigms, with classical conditioning relying on a temporal sequence of presentation, whereas operant conditioning embraces the variability in the temporal relationship between behavior and consequences. Exploring these nuances contributes to a comprehensive understanding of how organisms acquire and exhibit behaviors under varying environmental contexts, laying the groundwork for informed applications and interventions in diverse domains, including psychology, education, and behavioral therapies.

5. Nature and Role of Stimuli in Both Paradigms:

In the fields of both classical and operant conditioning, stimuli play a crucial role in shaping behavioral responses. Classical conditioning centers on the association between a previously neutral stimulus and an unconditioned stimulus to evoke a conditioned response. This process involves the identification and manipulation of stimuli to engender a specific behavioral reaction. In contrast, operant conditioning places emphasis on the role of stimuli in reinforcement and punishment processes, thereby influencing the occurrence and recurrence of behaviors. Understanding the nature and role of stimuli in both paradigms is integral to comprehending the mechanisms underpinning behavioral change.

Stimuli in classical conditioning are pivotal in establishing the conditioned response through the formation of associations. These stimuli act as triggers that elicit innate or reflexive responses, subsequently becoming linked to new, neutral stimuli. Recognition and differentiation of various types of stimuli are essential for the successful implementation of classical conditioning techniques. The role of timing and intensity of stimuli in classical conditioning is also a crucial aspect that influences the strength and persistence of conditioned responses. Additionally, the extinction of conditioned responses may occur when the conditioned stimulus is no longer paired with the unconditioned stimulus, highlighting the significance of stimuli in evoking and extinguishing learned responses.

In operant conditioning, stimuli serve as discriminative cues that signal the likelihood of reinforcement or punishment following a particular behavior. These stimuli provide information to the organism about the consequences of their actions, thereby influencing the probability of future occurrences of the behavior. Discriminative stimuli can include environmental cues that indicate when a certain behavior will be reinforced, shaping the individual's behavioral repertoire. Moreover, understanding the specific stimuli that function as reinforcers or punishers is imperative for effectively modifying and maintaining desired behaviors. The interplay of stimuli in both paradigms showcases the nature of behavioral conditioning and the multifaceted roles of stimuli in influencing behavioral outcomes.

6. Responses and Consequences:

Classical and operant conditioning operate on the fundamental principle of associative learning, but their distinction lies in the nature of the learned response and the role of consequences in shaping behavior. Classical conditioning primarily focuses on the involuntary and reflexive responses elicited by environmental stimuli. The conditioned stimulus (CS) becomes associated with the unconditioned stimulus (US), resulting in the conditioned response (CR). This process establishes a passive association between stimuli and responses, wherein the organism does not actively engage in producing the response.

On the other hand, operant conditioning centers on voluntary actions emitted by the organism, which are followed by certain consequences. These consequences can be reinforcing (increasing the likelihood of the behavior reoccurring) or punishing (decreasing the likelihood of the behavior reoccurring). The key distinction here is that the individual's behavior operates on the environment, and the subsequent consequences modulate the probability of that behavior occurring again.

In comparing these paradigms, it is evident that classical conditioning is more reactive in nature, while operant conditioning involves proactive, goal-directed behavior. Moreover, the role of consequences marks a significant disparity between the two paradigms. While classical conditioning emphasizes the association between stimuli, operant conditioning underscores the relationship between responses and their outcomes.

The timing of the stimuli and consequences differs in both paradigms. Classical conditioning predominantly deals with temporal contiguity, where the CS precedes the US, leading to the formation of associations between the two. In contrast, operant conditioning incorporates the concepts of reinforcement and punishment, with their precise timing critically influencing the effectiveness of modifying behavior.

7. Applications and Practical Implications:

The concepts of classical and operant conditioning have far-reaching implications in various domains, including education, therapy, organizational behavior, and everyday life. In educational settings, operant conditioning provides a powerful framework for understanding and influencing student behavior. By employing strategies such as positive reinforcement, educators can encourage desired behaviors and academic achievement. Conversely, an awareness of classical conditioning processes enables teachers to comprehend how past experiences may influence students' emotional responses and attitudes towards specific subjects or learning environments.

Within the field of therapy and mental health, the principles of both classical and operant conditioning inform therapeutic techniques aimed at addressing maladaptive behaviors and psychological disorders. For instance, systematic desensitization, a method based on classical conditioning, is frequently employed to alleviate phobias and anxiety by re-associating feared stimuli with relaxation or positive emotions. In behavioral therapy, operant conditioning principles are utilized to reinforce adaptive behaviors and extinguish harmful ones.

In organizational contexts, the application of operant conditioning principles can be observed in management strategies to motivate employees and shape workplace behaviors. Through the use of positive and negative reinforcement, organizations can effectively encourage desirable work practices and deter counterproductive behaviors. Additionally, an understanding of classical conditioning mechanisms can aid in comprehending how organizational culture, marketing efforts, and branding contribute to shaping consumer responses and associations.

Beyond these specific domains, the practical implications of these conditioning paradigms extend to various aspects of daily life. Parents, for example, can leverage operant conditioning techniques to promote positive behaviors in their children, while being mindful of inadvertent classical conditioning influences on their emotional development. Furthermore, understanding the principles of conditioning can heighten awareness of how media and advertising utilize these mechanisms to shape consumer preferences and purchasing behaviors.

8. Some Case Studies Illustrating Differences:

In the field of behavioral psychology, the application of classical and operant conditioning principles often presents intriguing nuances that manifest in various real-world scenarios. First and foremost, consider the case of an individual who develops an intense fear of flying subsequent to experiencing severe turbulence during a flight. Through the lens of classical conditioning, the individual's fear response becomes conditioned to the specific stimulus of flying, thereby mirroring the core tenets of Pavlov's pioneering experiments with dogs. This exemplifies the involuntary, reflexive nature of classical conditioning, wherein an innate or neutral stimulus becomes associated with an adverse emotional reaction.

Conversely, transitioning to operant conditioning, we encounter a distinct case that centers on employee performance within an organizational setting. Imagine a sales team operating under a reward-based system, where employees receive monetary bonuses for achieving or surpassing sales targets. By employing operant conditioning principles, the employees' behavior is shaped through positive reinforcement, as the desirable outcome (i.e., increased sales) elicits a favorable consequence (i.e., financial rewards). This starkly contrasts with the unbidden responses characteristic of classical conditioning, underscoring the deliberate, voluntary nature of operant behavioral modification.

Investigating the educational domain yields compelling insights into the divergence between these conditioning paradigms. Exploring a scenario within a classroom environment, we discern the application of classical conditioning in the emergence of a conditioned response among students. For instance, if a teacher consistently pairs a particular tone with the termination of a lecture, the students may develop an aversion to that tone, reflecting the acquisition of a conditioned response through association. In contrast, operant conditioning manifests when students exhibit enhanced participation in class discussions following the provision of praise or positive feedback, showcasing the shaping of voluntary behaviors based on consequences.

Behavioral Responses - Types and Patterns

1. Innate vs. Learned Behaviors:

In the field of behavioral responses, a fundamental distinction lies in the differentiation between innate and learned behaviors. Innate behaviors, also referred to as instinctive behaviors, are those that an organism exhibits naturally without the need for prior experience or environmental influence. These behaviors are often crucial for survival and are genetically hardwired into the organism's biological makeup. Examples of innate behaviors include reflexes, such as the knee-jerk reflex, and innate defensive behaviors exhibited by prey animals when faced with a predator.

Contrastingly, learned behaviors are the product of an organism's interaction with its environment through experiences, observations, and conditioning. These behaviors are acquired through practice, repetition, and association with specific stimuli or situations. Learning can occur through various mechanisms, including classical conditioning, operant conditioning, observation, and cognitive processes. For instance, a dog learning to sit on command through consistent training and reinforcement demonstrates a learned behavior.

Understanding the differences between innate and learned behaviors is integral to comprehending the adaptive capabilities of organisms and the interplay between genetics and environment in shaping behavior. It also sheds light on the plasticity and malleability of behavior, emphasizing the role of experience and environmental factors in modifying and developing new behavioral patterns.

The distinction between innate and learned behaviors carries significant implications across diverse fields, including psychology, ethology, and evolutionary biology. Researchers studying animal behavior often investigate the balance between instinctual behaviors crucial for species survival and the behavioral flexibility conferred by learning. This intersection offers valuable insights into the evolution of behaviors and the adaptive advantages conferred by the ability to acquire and modify behavioral responses.

Understanding innate and learned behaviors is pertinent to applied domains such as education, therapy, and animal training. Educators leverage knowledge of learning principles to optimize instructional strategies, while therapists utilize behavior modification techniques to address maladaptive learned behaviors. Similarly, trainers employ conditioning methods to cultivate desired behaviors in animals, leveraging the principles of reinforcement and shaping.

2. Behavioral Patterns - Fixed and Variable:

In the context of operant conditioning, behavioral patterns are often categorized as either fixed or variable. Fixed behavioral patterns refer to responses that occur at a consistent rate or intensity, while variable behavioral patterns involve responses that fluctuate in terms of frequency or strength.

Fixed behavioral patterns are characterized by a stable and predictable occurrence of behavior. This type of pattern is commonly observed in behaviors that are highly ingrained or routine, such as reflexive responses or well-practiced actions. For example, the act of blinking in response to a sudden bright light can be considered a fixed behavioral pattern due to its consistent and involuntary nature.

On the other hand, variable behavioral patterns encompass behaviors that display variability in their occurrence. These responses may fluctuate in frequency, duration, or intensity based on internal or external factors. Variable behavioral patterns are often associated with more complex and adaptable behaviors, including those influenced by motivation, environmental cues, or learning experiences.

Understanding the distinction between fixed and variable behavioral patterns is essential for designing effective reinforcement and intervention strategies. Fixed patterns may benefit from consistent reinforcement schedules to maintain the desired behavior, whereas variable patterns may require adaptive reinforcement techniques to account for fluctuations in response strength or occurrence.

The study of behavioral patterns provides valuable insights into the underlying mechanisms of behavior and the influence of environmental contingencies. By analyzing fixed and variable patterns across diverse behaviors, researchers and practitioners can gain a deeper understanding of the factors shaping human and animal behavior, leading to more precise and targeted interventions in educational, clinical, and organizational settings.

3. The Concept of Response Classes:

A response class refers to a group of responses that all produce the same effect on the environment. These responses may vary widely in their topography or form, but share common functions and outcomes. In essence, response classes provide a framework for categorizing behaviors based on their shared consequences, allowing for more comprehensive analysis of behavior patterns.

Understanding response classes is crucial for behavior analysts and researchers as it enables them to identify the functional relationships between behavior and its consequences. By grouping similar responses together, analysts can identify broader patterns and trends in behavior, providing valuable insights into the underlying mechanisms driving specific behavioral outcomes.

Response classes can encompass a wide range of behaviors, from simple motor actions to complex cognitive processes. For example, in a classroom setting, raising one's hand to answer a question, speaking out of turn, or quietly participating could all belong to the same response class if they lead to similar consequences, such as attention from the teacher or approval from peers. By recognizing these behaviors as part of a response class, educators can develop targeted interventions to shape desirable behaviors and reduce undesirable ones.

The concept of response classes underscores the importance of considering the broader context in which behaviors occur. Analyzing behaviors within the framework of response classes allows for a more holistic understanding of behavior, accounting for the diversity of responses that lead to similar outcomes. This comprehensive approach can reveal patterns of behavior and shed light on the factors influencing behavioral consistency or variability.

The practical applications of understanding response classes extend beyond the field of research and academia. In clinical settings, identifying response classes is pivotal for designing effective behavior modification programs, as it allows professionals to tailor interventions to address specific response patterns. By targeting entire response classes rather than individual behaviors, practitioners can develop comprehensive strategies to promote positive change and address problematic behaviors effectively.

4. Analysis of Response Chains:

A response chain refers to a series of individual behaviors that occur successively, each serving as a cue or signal for the next behavior in the sequence. This concept is integral to comprehending how certain behaviors are elicited and maintained through reinforcement.

The analysis of response chains involves dissecting the behavioral sequences into their constituent parts. Each component behavior in the chain can be identified and analyzed in terms of its antecedents, consequences, and the relations between preceding and subsequent behaviors. By examining these sequences, researchers can gain insight into the specific triggers and reinforcements that lead to the completion of the entire response chain.

Understanding response chains is crucial in various fields, including psychology, education, and behavioral therapy. For instance, in educational settings, educators often utilize response chains to teach complex skills such as problem-solving or decision-making. By breaking down the desired skill into smaller, manageable steps, instructors can effectively guide learners through the sequential behaviors necessary for mastery. Moreover, in therapeutic interventions, the analysis of response chains is employed to address maladaptive or harmful behaviors by identifying the points at which intervention can disrupt the chain and promote more adaptive responses.

The analysis of response chains enables the development of effective behavior modification strategies. By identifying specific points within the chain where reinforcement can be implemented, behavior analysts can design targeted interventions to shape and strengthen desired behavioral sequences. In doing so, they can systematically modify and shape behavior to achieve desired outcomes, whether in clinical or organizational contexts.

Researchers also examine response chains to explore the impact of environmental stimuli and situational variables on behavior. By observing how different stimuli influence the initiation and progression of response chains, psychologists can gain valuable insights into the factors that contribute to the maintenance or alteration of behavioral patterns.

5. Impact of Schedules on Behavior:

In operant conditioning, the impact of schedules on behavior is a critical aspect that warrants comprehensive understanding. Schedules of reinforcement and punishment play a pivotal role in shaping and maintaining behavioral responses. These schedules can be classified into two main categories: continuous and intermittent.

Continuous schedules involve reinforcing or punishing an individual's behavior every time it occurs. Such schedules are effective in establishing new behaviors, as they provide clear associations between the behavior and its consequences. However, continuous reinforcement may not always be feasible or practical in real-world settings.

Intermittent schedules, on the other hand, involve reinforcing or punishing behavior intermittently or periodically. There are several types of intermittent schedules, including fixed ratio (FR), variable ratio (VR), fixed interval (FI), and variable interval (VI). Each type has distinct effects on behavior.

Fixed ratio schedules reinforce behavior after a specific number of responses. They typically result in high rates of responding, as individuals strive to achieve the required number of responses for reinforcement. Variable ratio schedules, on the other hand, provide reinforcement after an unpredictable number of responses, leading to persistent and consistent behavioral responses.

Fixed interval schedules reinforce the first response after a fixed period of time has elapsed since the previous reinforcement. This often results in a pattern of behavior where there is a lull in responding immediately after reinforcement, followed by an increase in responding as the time for the next reinforcement approaches. Variable interval schedules reinforce the first response after a varying amount of time has passed, leading to steady but moderate rates of responding.

6. Adaptive and Maladaptive Behavior Patterns:

Understanding the distinction between adaptive and maladaptive Behavior is crucial for comprehending how individuals interact with their environment and learn new behaviors. Adaptive behavior patterns refer to those actions that enable an individual to effectively thrive within their environment. These behaviors are considered beneficial and constructive, as they contribute to an individual's ability to meet their needs and achieve personal goals. On the other hand, maladaptive behavior patterns encompass actions that hinder an individual's functioning or well-being. Such behaviors are often counterproductive, leading to negative outcomes and interfering with an individual's ability to fulfill their potential. Identifying and analyzing adaptive and maladaptive behavior patterns provides valuable insights into the underlying mechanisms of behavior and the factors influencing behavioral change. Additionally, recognizing these patterns is essential for developing effective behavior modification strategies aimed at promoting adaptive behaviors and reducing maladaptive ones. In the context of operant conditioning, the reinforcement or punishment of specific behaviors can significantly impact whether these behaviors become adaptive or maladaptive. By examining real-world examples and case studies, we can gain a deeper understanding of the complexities involved in differentiating between adaptive and maladaptive behavior patterns. Moreover, exploring the underlying motivations and consequences of these patterns allows us to appreciate the interplay between individual behaviors, environmental stimuli, and the reinforcing or punishing contingencies that shape behavior. As we delve into the nuanced dynamics of adaptive and maladaptive behavior patterns, we uncover the multifaceted nature of human behavior and its remarkable capacity for adaptation and change.

7. Measuring and Recording Behavioral Responses:

In order to understand the complex nature of behavioral responses, meticulous measurement and recording of behavioral responses are integral to understanding the complexities of human and animal behaviors. This process involves systematic observation and data collection to capture the nuances and variations in behavior. One of the fundamental aspects of measuring behavioral responses is to establish clear operational definitions for the behaviors being studied. This enables researchers to precisely identify and classify the actions being exhibited by the subjects under scrutiny.

Various methods are employed to measure and record behavioral responses, each with its own advantages and limitations. Direct observation entails physically witnessing and documenting the behaviors as they occur, allowing for real-time data gathering. Alternatively, technology-driven approaches such as video recording and motion sensors offer a more precise and detailed analysis of behaviors, enabling researchers to review and analyze the responses repeatedly to discern patterns and trends.

In addition to direct observation, self-reports and interviews can be utilized to gather introspective data on subjective behaviors, thoughts, and feelings. While this method provides valuable insight into the internal processes underlying behavior, it is crucial to consider potential biases and discrepancies that may arise from self-reporting.

Once the data is collected, it is imperative to employ reliable and valid measurement instruments to accurately quantify and record the behavioral responses. These instruments range from simple checklists and rating scales to sophisticated electronic devices designed to capture specific behavioral parameters. The choice of measurement instrument is contingent upon the nature of the behaviors being studied and the research objectives.

Recording behavioral responses necessitates organizing and categorizing the gathered data efficiently. This involves creating detailed behavioral records that encompass the frequency, duration, intensity, and latency of the observed behaviors. Additionally, employing systematic sampling techniques allows for the collection of representative data while minimizing observer bias.

The role of context and environmental factors cannot be overlooked when measuring and recording behavioral responses. It is essential to consider the situational and contextual variables that may influence behavior, as well as the impact of social and cultural factors on behavioral patterns.

8. Influence of External Stimuli on Response Types:

External stimuli can encompass a wide array of environmental cues, including but not limited to sensory inputs, social interactions, and situational contexts. Understanding how external stimuli influence response types is crucial in elucidating the complexities of behavior and the mechanisms through which behavioral patterns manifest in various settings.

The impact of external stimuli on response types can be observed across different domains, from simple reflexive reactions to more learned behaviors. For instance, in a laboratory setting, an individual may display specific responses when presented with varying auditory or visual cues, highlighting the significance of external stimuli in evoking distinct behavioral reactions. Similarly, in daily life, individuals exhibit varying responses to social situations, influenced by external cues such as verbal communication, body language, and environmental conditions.

The influence of external stimuli on response types extends beyond immediate behavioral manifestations. Environmental cues can serve as discriminative stimuli, signaling the likelihood of reinforcement or punishment associated with specific behaviors. Through processes of stimulus generalization and discrimination, individuals learn to differentiate between contextual cues and adjust their responses accordingly, illustrating the profound impact of external stimuli on the modulation of behavior.

An in-depth exploration of the influence of external stimuli on response types also necessitates an examination of individual differences in responsiveness to environmental cues. Factors such as past experiences, genetic predispositions, and social learning greatly contribute to the variability in how individuals perceive and respond to external stimuli. Understanding these individual differences enhances our comprehension of the multifaceted nature of behavioral responses and emphasizes the need for personalized approaches in behavioral interventions and modifications.

Principles of Behavioral Modification

1. Introduction:

The historical perspective of behavioral modification dates back to early studies conducted by behaviorists such as B.F. Skinner, Ivan Pavlov, and John B. Watson, who laid the foundation for understanding the principles of learning and behavior. These early pioneers emphasized the importance of environmental factors in shaping behavior and demonstrated the potential for behavior modification through conditioning. The development of behavioral modification has been influenced by various theoretical approaches, including operant conditioning and classical conditioning, which have provided valuable insights into the mechanisms of behavior change.

At its core, behavioral modification aims to bring about desirable changes in an individual's behavior by employing systematic techniques derived from empirical findings and theoretical frameworks. It emphasizes the use of positive reinforcement, negative reinforcement, and punishment as tools for shaping and controlling behavior. Behavioral modification also considers factors such as motivation, cognition, and emotion in the process of behavior change, highlighting the multifaceted nature of human behavior. Furthermore, it takes into account the role of social and cultural influences on behavior, recognizing the complex interplay between individual and environmental determinants.

The objectives of behavioral modification encompass a wide range of applications, including clinical psychology, education, organizational management, and personal development. In clinical settings, behavioral modification interventions are utilized to treat various mental health disorders, address maladaptive behaviors, and promote overall well-being. Within educational contexts, behavioral modification strategies are employed to enhance learning outcomes, manage classroom behaviors, and support students with diverse needs. In organizational settings, behavioral modification techniques are implemented to improve employee performance, foster a positive work environment, and facilitate organizational change. Additionally, individuals seek behavioral modification to attain personal growth, overcome unhealthy habits, and achieve their goals.

2. Historical Perspectives and Development:

The historical evolution of behavioral modification can be traced back to the early 20th century. Notably, the work of B.F. Skinner played a pivotal role in shaping the foundations of behavioral modification. Skinner's research and experiments with operant conditioning laid the groundwork for the systematic analysis and modification of behavior. His conceptualization of reinforcement and punishment as crucial determinants of behavior has had a profound impact on the field. The subsequent refinement of these concepts by prominent behaviorists such as E. L. Thorndike and John B. Watson further propelled the development of behavioral modification.

The mid-20th century witnessed substantial advancements in the application of behavioral modification techniques across various domains, including clinical psychology, education, and organizational management. This era saw the emergence of behavior therapy as a distinct therapeutic approach, with influential figures like Joseph Wolpe and Albert Bandura contributing significantly to its theoretical and applied aspects. Their pioneering work laid the groundwork for the effective treatment of maladaptive behaviors and psychological disorders through behavioral interventions.

In the latter half of the 20th century, the integration of behavioral modification with cognitive psychology gave rise to cognitive-behavioral approaches, which combined the principles of behaviorism with cognitive restructuring techniques. This integration broadened the scope of behavioral modification, allowing for a more comprehensive understanding of human behavior and cognition. The advent of technology further revolutionized the field, providing innovative tools and methodologies for behavior assessment, intervention, and monitoring. As the field continues to evolve, contemporary developments in neuroscience and biobehavioral research are shedding new light on the mechanisms underlying behavioral modification. With the interdisciplinary collaboration between psychology, neuroscience, and related fields, the future holds promising prospects for advancing the efficacy and precision of behavioral modification techniques.

3. Core Principles of Behavioral Analysis:

The fundamental principle of behavioral analysis is the emphasis on observable behaviors as the primary focus of study, rather than relying on subjective interpretations or internal mental processes. This approach allows for the precise measurement and examination of behavior in specific contexts, leading to a more systematic understanding of behavioral patterns. Additionally, behavioral analysis acknowledges the influence of environmental factors, including antecedents and consequences, in shaping and maintaining behaviors. By identifying the environmental determinants of behavior, practitioners can devise targeted interventions to modify and reinforce desirable behaviors while minimizing undesirable ones. Another key principle is the concept of functional relationships between behaviors and their consequences, which highlights the cause-and-effect dynamics that govern behavioral responses. Understanding these relationships enables practitioners to implement strategic reinforcement and punishment techniques effectively. Moreover, behavioral analysis emphasizes the significance of individual differences in responding to environmental stimuli and learning experiences, recognizing that personalized approaches are essential for successful behavior modification. This principle underscores the need for tailored intervention strategies based on an individual's unique characteristics and history. Furthermore, the principle of empirical validation is central to behavioral analysis, advocating for the use of evidence-based methods to assess the effectiveness of behavior modification interventions. Rigorous empirical research and data-driven evaluation contribute to the advancement of behavioral analysis and its applications in diverse settings. Lastly, ethical considerations form an integral part of behavioral analysis, guiding practitioners in upholding professional standards and safeguarding the well-being and autonomy of those undergoing behavior modification. Adhering to ethical guidelines ensures that interventions prioritize the welfare and dignity of individuals, promoting responsible and respectful practices in the field of behavioral analysis. A thorough grasp of these fundamental principles is indispensable for practitioners engaged in behavioral modification endeavors.

4. Reinforcement Strategies for Behavior Change:

The application of positive reinforcement, wherein desirable behaviors are rewarded with positive stimuli, serves as an effective means to increase the likelihood of those behaviors recurring. Tangible rewards such as tokens, prizes, or privileges are often utilized to reinforce positive behavior in educational and therapeutic contexts, fostering motivation and engagement. Furthermore, social reinforcers, including verbal praise, encouragement, and recognition, can significantly impact behavior, serving as powerful tools in promoting desired conduct. Conversely, negative reinforcement involves the removal of aversive stimuli following the display of the target behavior, thereby strengthening the likelihood of its occurrence in the future. The strategic implementation of negative reinforcement in behavior modification programs necessitates careful consideration of individual preferences and sensitivities to ensure ethical and effective practice. Understanding the principles of reinforcement schedules is paramount in optimizing behavior change interventions. Whether employing continuous reinforcement, which provides reinforcement following every instance of the targeted behavior, or intermittent reinforcement, where reinforcement is administered periodically, the choice of schedule is tailored to the specific behavioral goals and the individual's responsiveness. Moreover, the differentiation between fixed ratio, variable ratio, fixed interval, and variable interval schedules holds considerable significance in shaping sustained behavioral patterns. Behavioral modification practitioners analyze these schedules to tailor reinforcement strategies that maximize the desired outcomes while minimizing the risk of extinction or undesired side effects. It is essential to recognize that the effectiveness of reinforcement strategies is contingent upon individual variability, necessitating ongoing assessment and adaptation. As such, the personalized nature of reinforcement application calls for collaboration among professionals, caregivers, and individuals undergoing behavioral modification, ensuring a cohesive, multi-dimensional approach to fostering lasting behavioral change.

5. Application of Punishment in Behavior Management:

Punishment is a controversial aspect of behavior management, integral to the broader framework of operant conditioning. It encompasses the application of aversive stimuli or the removal of positive reinforcements with the aim of decreasing the probability of targeted behaviors. Effective utilization of punishment strategies requires a deep understanding of its implications and considerations.

It is essential to differentiate between positive punishment, involving the introduction of an adverse stimulus in response to a behavior, and negative punishment, which entails the removal of a valued stimulus as a consequence of the behavior. Additionally, the timing and consistency of applying punishment play pivotal roles in its efficacy. Inappropriate or erratic implementation of punishment can lead to unintended outcomes, including heightened aggression, fear, or the development of avoidance behaviors.

Careful consideration must be given to the ethical dimensions of punishment-based interventions. The potential for adverse emotional and psychological impacts on individuals subject to punitive measures necessitates a delicate balance between achieving behavioral change and preserving overall well-being. Furthermore, the long-term effects of punishment, including its potential to suppress behavior temporarily rather than engender sustained modification, necessitate cautious implementation.

Behavioral managers should maintain a comprehensive repertoire of alternative strategies and interventions, utilizing punishment sparingly and judiciously. Crucially, a proactive approach that emphasizes positive reinforcement and the promotion of desirable behaviors often proves more effective in fostering lasting change while minimizing adverse repercussions. When applied discriminately and in alignment with ethical guidelines, punishment can serve as a valuable tool within the broader spectrum of behavior management. The responsibility lies with practitioners and professionals to apply punitive measures ethically and responsibly, always mindful of the potential ramifications on individual well-being.

6. Role of Stimulus Control in Behavioral Adjustment:

Stimulus control refers to the influence of discriminative stimuli on an individual's behavior, essentially determining when certain behaviors will be reinforced or not. Understanding the role of stimulus control is crucial for effectively modifying behavior, as it allows practitioners to identify the specific environmental cues that trigger certain responses.

In practice, stimulus control involves the process of discrimination training, where an individual learns to respond to specific cues or signals while suppressing responses in the absence of these cues. By systematically reinforcing behaviors only in the presence of particular stimuli, individuals become more adept at discriminating when to perform a certain behavior, leading to improved behavioral adjustment.

Stimulus control also encompasses the concept of generalization, whereby the individual exhibits the desired behavior in settings or situations beyond those where the behavior was initially learned or reinforced. This generalization of behavior is a key indicator of successful behavior modification, indicating that the individual has effectively associated the behavior with a broad range of relevant stimuli.

The role of stimulus control extends beyond simple associations between cues and behaviors, delving into the complexities of contextual and discriminative stimuli. It requires careful analysis of the environmental factors that elicit or inhibit certain behaviors, allowing for targeted interventions aimed at promoting adaptive responses and reducing maladaptive behaviors.

Practitioners must also consider the potential for stimulus discrimination, where individuals may struggle to differentiate between similar stimuli, leading to inconsistencies in their behavioral responses. Addressing stimulus discrimination challenges through focused training and reinforcement techniques is integral to refining an individual's ability to accurately discriminate between relevant stimuli and appropriately adjust their behavior.

Understanding stimulus control is essential for addressing issues related to stimulus generalization, where individuals may exhibit the desired behavior in the presence of irrelevant but similar stimuli. Techniques such as fading, which involves gradually reducing the salience of discriminative stimuli, can help individuals to exhibit the target behavior specifically in response to the intended cues, enhancing the precision of behavioral adjustment.

7. Techniques in Behavioral Modification:

Shaping and chaining are fundamental techniques employed in behavioral modification to enable the development of complex behaviors through a systematic process of reinforcement. Shaping involves successive approximations towards a desired behavior, where initially, any approximation or aspect of the target behavior is reinforced, and over time, only closer approximations are reinforced until the final behavior is achieved. This gradual shaping allows individuals to exhibit behaviors that might not initially be present in their repertoire. It is a powerful tool for developing new behaviors or refining existing ones. Chaining, on the other hand, involves breaking down a complex behavior into smaller, more manageable components, which are then taught and linked together to form the complete behavioral sequence. This technique is particularly useful when attempting to teach individuals a series of actions or responses in a specific order. By reinforcing each link in the chain, the individual learns to perform the entire sequence. Understanding the concepts of shaping and chaining is crucial for practitioners of behavioral modification as it provides the framework for systematically guiding behavior towards desired outcomes. The application of these techniques requires careful planning, clear identification of target behaviors, and consistent reinforcement of progress. Furthermore, the ability to effectively shape and chain behaviors necessitates a deep understanding of individual differences, motivation, and learning styles. Successful implementation of these techniques also demands astute observation skills, as practitioners must be able to recognize and reinforce the smallest steps towards the desired behavior. Additionally, consideration of task complexity, frequency and timing of reinforcements, and potential variations in environmental conditions is paramount. Sustained use of shaping and chaining can lead to significant changes in behavior, ultimately contributing to the overall success of behavioral modification interventions. Importantly, the ethical implications of utilizing these techniques should be carefully considered, ensuring that individuals' dignity and autonomy are respected throughout the shaping and chaining process.

8. Generalization and Discrimination:

Generalization and discrimination play a significant role in understanding how behaviors are learned and maintained. Generalization refers to the process by which an individual exhibits a learned response to similar stimuli that were present during the original learning experience. In other words, it involves the extension of a learned behavior to new stimuli or situations that share similarities with the original learning context. For instance, if a child learns to say 'please' when asking for something at home, they might generalize this polite behavior to other settings such as school or the grocery store. Understanding generalization allows behavior modification practitioners to anticipate how learned behaviors might manifest in various real-world contexts. On the other hand, discrimination is the ability to differentiate between similar but distinct stimuli and respond differently to each. Applied to behavior modification, discrimination training involves teaching individuals to exhibit specific responses only in the presence of certain stimuli while withholding those responses in the presence of others. This skill is crucial for helping individuals adapt to diverse environments and social settings, ensuring that appropriate behaviors are displayed in specific situations. Furthermore, understanding discrimination is essential for addressing issues such as overgeneralization, where an individual may inappropriately apply a learned behavior to unrelated contexts. To promote effective discrimination, behavior modification programs often include systematic training procedures that involve gradually introducing and reinforcing discernment between relevant stimuli. As behavior modification practitioners delve into the complexities of generalization and discrimination, they must consider the influence of factors such as reinforcement history, stimulus salience, and contextual cues on the process of learning and responding. Additionally, recognizing the interplay between these concepts contributes to the development of targeted intervention strategies aimed at promoting desired behaviors while minimizing undesirable responses in diverse settings. While generalization and discrimination represent aspects of behavioral modification, mastering these principles empowers us to design comprehensive and adaptive interventions that optimize behavior change outcomes for individuals across various life domains.

9. Ethical Considerations in Behavioral Modification Practices:

Ethical considerations are paramount in the field of behavioral modification practices, as they directly impact the well-being and rights of individuals undergoing such interventions. One of the primary ethical principles underlying behavioral modification is the concept of informed consent. It is imperative that individuals or their legal guardians are fully informed about the nature, purpose, risks, and potential benefits of any behavior modification program before providing consent to participate.

Practitioners of behavioral modification must ensure that their interventions are based on sound scientific evidence and best practices. This involves conducting comprehensive assessments, utilizing validated assessment tools, and employing interventions with demonstrated efficacy and safety. Practitioners should also stay informed about the latest research and developments in the field to continually enhance the quality of their services and minimize any potential harm to their clients.

In addition, privacy and confidentiality are crucial ethical considerations in behavioral modification practices. Clients have the right to expect that their personal information will be kept confidential, and practitioners must take appropriate measures to safeguard this information. This includes obtaining explicit consent before sharing any client-related information with third parties and explaining the limits of confidentiality to clients at the outset of the intervention.

Another critical ethical facet is the avoidance of coercion and undue influence in behavioral modification programs. It is essential for practitioners to create an environment where clients feel empowered to make autonomous decisions about their participation in the program. This requires transparent communication, respect for autonomy, and a focus on the individual's best interests.

Cultural competence and sensitivity to diversity must be integrated into behavioral modification practices to ensure that interventions are responsive to the unique needs, values, and beliefs of diverse populations. Practitioners should strive to provide culturally sensitive services and adapt their approaches to align with the cultural backgrounds and preferences of their clients.

Lastly, ongoing evaluation and monitoring of ethical standards within behavioral modification practices are indispensable. This involves establishing clear policies and procedures for addressing ethical concerns, providing ethics training for practitioners, and creating avenues for clients to voice grievances or concerns regarding ethical conduct. By upholding these ethical considerations, practitioners can cultivate an environment of trust, respect, and integrity within the field of behavioral modification.

Mechanisms Underpinning Behavioral Change

1. Introduction to Behavioral Change Mechanisms:

Behavioral change mechanisms are at the core of understanding human behavior and the processes involved in modifying and shaping it. In the field of psychology, an array of foundational theories and models have been developed to explain the underlying mechanisms that drive behavioral change. These theories serve as frameworks for comprehending the complexities of human behavior and provide insight into how individuals learn new behaviors, adapt to their environments, and modify existing patterns of action.

One of the most influential theories in this domain is the Social Learning Theory proposed by Albert Bandura. This theory emphasizes the role of observation and imitation in the acquisition and modification of behaviors. Bandura's concept of self-efficacy also underscores the individual's belief in their own capability to master tasks and achieve goals, which has profound implications for behavioral change interventions.

The Health Belief Model, developed by social psychologists Hochbaum, Rosenstock, and Kegels in the 1950s, explores the factors influencing people’s decision-making processes about their health behaviors. This model identifies cues to action, perceived susceptibility, perceived severity, perceived benefits, and perceived barriers as key components affecting health-related behavioral change, thus providing a valuable framework for researchers and practitioners working in health psychology contexts.

In addition, the Transtheoretical Model of Behavior Change, commonly known as the Stages of Change Model, delineates distinct stages individuals progress through when modifying behaviors. The model identifies pre-contemplation, contemplation, preparation, action, and maintenance as sequential stages involved in bringing about lasting changes in behavior. Understanding these stages can inform the development of tailored interventions that effectively support individuals at different points in their behavior change journey.

Another pivotal theory is the Theory of Planned Behavior, which posits that an individual's intention is the most immediate determinant of their behavior. This model takes into account an individual's attitude, subjective norms, and perceived behavioral control in predicting behavioral intentions and subsequent change. Thus, the theory provides actionable insights for strategizing interventions towards fostering behavioral change.

These foundational theories and models play a crucial role in informing research, clinical practice, and public health efforts aimed at influencing and facilitating behavioral change across various domains of human activity.

2. Neuroscientific Perspectives on Behavior Modification:

Behavior modification is a complex process that can be better understood through the lens of neuroscientific perspectives. The study of how the brain and nervous system impact behavior provides valuable insights into the mechanisms underlying behavioral change. Neuroimaging techniques, such as functional magnetic resonance imaging (fMRI) and positron emission tomography (PET), have allowed researchers to observe and analyze brain activity associated with different behaviors. This has revealed the involvement of various brain regions and neurotransmitter systems in mediating behavioral responses. For example, studies have shown that decision-making processes and reward-related behaviors are associated with the activity of the dopaminergic system in the brain's reward pathway. Understanding these neurochemical mechanisms can inform the development of targeted interventions for behavior modification. Additionally, advances in neuroplasticity research have highlighted the brain's remarkable ability to reorganize itself in response to experience. This phenomenon underscores the potential for individuals to learn new behaviors and habits through intentional training and repetition. Furthermore, insights from studies on neural connectivity and network dynamics shed light on how different brain regions communicate and coordinate to produce and modify behavior. Mapping these networks can provide a roadmap for understanding the neural basis of maladaptive behaviors and devising strategies for their alteration. By unraveling the neuroscientific underpinnings of behavior modification, researchers and practitioners can tailor interventions to target specific neural pathways and optimize the likelihood of successful change. Moreover, this knowledge can help in developing personalized approaches that consider individual differences in brain function and structure. Ultimately, integrating neuroscientific perspectives into the study of behavior modification offers promising avenues for enhancing the effectiveness of interventions and promoting enduring behavioral change.

3. The Role of Genetic Predispositions:

The field of behavioral genetics has demonstrated that certain genetic variations can influence an individual's susceptibility to specific behavioral traits and tendencies. These predispositions, often inherited from one's parents, can impact an individual's likelihood to exhibit certain behaviors or respond to environmental triggers in distinct ways.

Researchers have identified specific genes associated with behavioral traits such as impulsivity, aggression, and susceptibility to addiction. While genetic predispositions do not dictate one's behavior outright, they can significantly influence the likelihood of developing particular behavioral patterns in response to environmental factors.

Understanding the interplay between genetic predispositions and environmental influences is critical in comprehending the nuanced nature of behavioral change. It is important to acknowledge that genetic predispositions provide a foundational framework that interacts with environmental stimuli to shape an individual's behavioral responses. For instance, individuals with a genetic predisposition for impulsivity may be more prone to impulsive behaviors when exposed to certain environmental stressors.

The study of epigenetics has revealed the dynamic nature of genetic predispositions, highlighting how environmental factors can influence gene expression and subsequently alter behavioral outcomes. This interplay between genetics and environment underscores the complexity of behavioral change mechanisms, emphasizing the need for a comprehensive approach that integrates both genetic and environmental factors.

Recognizing genetic predispositions can have profound implications for behavioral interventions and therapeutic approaches. By understanding an individual's genetic predispositions, tailored interventions can be designed to target specific behavioral tendencies, optimizing the effectiveness of behavior modification strategies.

4. Environmental Factors Influencing Behavior:

The external environment, including social, cultural, and physical surroundings, significantly impacts an individual's behavior. Social environments, such as family dynamics, peer relationships, and societal norms, can exert profound influence on an individual's actions and choices. For instance, the presence of nurturing and supportive interpersonal relationships can foster positive behaviors, while adverse social environments may contribute to the development of maladaptive patterns. Similarly, cultural expectations and values prevalent in a community can shape an individual's behavior by providing normative guidelines for acceptable conduct. Physical surroundings, including access to resources, infrastructure, and natural settings, also influence behavior. Resource-rich environments may promote pro-social behaviors, while resource-scarce environments can lead to competitive or even aggressive behavioral expressions. Moreover, the design and layout of physical spaces, such as urban planning and architectural features, can impact human behavior. For example, well-designed public spaces may encourage cooperation and engagement, whereas poorly planned environments may foster feelings of isolation and disconnection. Furthermore, exposure to environmental stressors, such as pollution, noise, or overcrowding, can trigger negative behavioral responses and affect mental well-being. Understanding the multifaceted impact of environmental factors on behavior is essential for implementing effective behavior modification strategies.

5. Synaptic Plasticity and Learning:

Synaptic plasticity, a fundamental process in the brain, involves the ability of synapses to strengthen or weaken over time, thereby influencing the transmission of signals between neurons. In the context of operant conditioning, synaptic plasticity is essential for encoding new behavioral responses and modifying existing ones.

At the cellular level, mechanisms such as long-term potentiation (LTP) and long-term depression (LTD) are crucial in synaptic plasticity. LTP refers to the persistent strengthening of synaptic connections, which is associated with the enhancement of neural communication and the consolidation of memory representations. Conversely, LTD involves the weakening of synaptic transmission, enabling the brain to prune unnecessary connections and refine its neural circuits.

The phenomenon of synaptic plasticity aligns closely with the principles of operant conditioning, as it underpins the neurobiological basis of learning through reinforcement and punishment. When a specific behavior is reinforced, such as through positive reinforcement in operant conditioning, the associated neural pathways undergo synaptic changes, leading to a potentiation of the connections involved in mediating that behavior. On the other hand, punishment may lead to the weakening of synaptic connections, discouraging the recurrence of the targeted behavior.

The concept of metaplasticity, or the plasticity of synaptic plasticity, sheds light on the dynamic nature of synaptic changes in response to previous experiences. This adaptive feature allows the brain to adjust its plasticity mechanisms based on prior environmental and behavioral factors, enhancing its capacity to learn and adapt to new stimuli. As operant conditioning relies on the modification of behavior through consequences, the interplay between synaptic plasticity and metaplasticity serves as the neural substrate for the acquisition and refinement of conditioned responses.

Understanding the relationship between synaptic plasticity and operant conditioning elucidates how the brain's ability to rewire its circuitry in response to reinforcement, punishment, and environmental cues translates into the acquisition and expression of adaptive behaviors. Moreover, advances in research on synaptic plasticity offer promising avenues for developing interventions aimed at optimizing learning processes and mitigating maladaptive behaviors.

6. Cognitive Processes in Operant Conditioning:

Cognitive processes influence how individuals perceive, interpret, and respond to environmental stimuli. In the context of behavior modification, cognitive factors contribute to the acquisition, maintenance, and extinction of learned behaviors. One key aspect of cognitive processes in operant conditioning is the individual's attention to environmental cues and the subsequent encoding of relevant information. This selective attention shapes which stimuli are more likely to elicit behavioral responses, thus impacting the reinforcement or punishment of specific behaviors.

Cognitive processes encompass the mental representation of desired outcomes and the evaluation of potential actions to achieve these goals. Individuals engage in internal deliberation and decision-making processes based on their understanding of the consequences associated with different behaviors. This cognitive assessment influences the likelihood of engaging in specific behaviors and the responsiveness to reinforcement and punishment.

Cognitive processes contribute to the generalization and discrimination of learned behaviors. Through cognitive categorization, individuals distinguish between various contextual cues and determine the appropriateness of particular behavioral responses in different situations. This cognitive flexibility allows for adaptive behavioral adjustments and the modulation of responses based on changing environmental contingencies.

Additionally, cognitive factors influence the self-regulation of behavior, including aspects such as goal setting, self-monitoring, and self-evaluation. These metacognitive processes enable individuals to regulate and modify their own behaviors by setting attainable goals, monitoring progress, and adjusting strategies based on feedback and internal reflection. Self-regulation is particularly significant in sustaining long-term behavioral changes and preventing relapse.

7. Emotional Regulators and Their Influence on Behavior:

Emotions play a significant role in shaping human behavior and responses to stimuli. The interplay between emotional states and behavioral outcomes is a complex yet integral aspect of operant conditioning. Emotional regulators such as fear, joy, anger, and sadness can profoundly influence an individual's behavioral repertoire. Understanding the mechanisms through which emotions impact behavior is essential for comprehending the intricacies of operant conditioning processes. Emotional regulation involves the ability to recognize and manage one's emotional responses, which in turn shapes behavioral patterns. Research in psychology and neuroscience has shed light on the neural pathways and brain regions involved in emotional regulation and its impact on behavior. The amygdala, prefrontal cortex, and hippocampus are key areas implicated in modulating emotional responses and subsequent behavioral adaptations. Moreover, the interaction between neurotransmitters such as serotonin, dopamine, and norepinephrine further elucidates the link between emotional states and behavioral choices. Furthermore, social and environmental factors contribute significantly to the regulation of emotions and, consequently, behavioral alterations. The presence of supportive social networks, positive reinforcement from peers, and exposure to enriching environments can enhance emotional regulation abilities and foster more adaptive behaviors. Conversely, adverse social contexts and chronic stress may lead to dysregulated emotional states, resulting in maladaptive behaviors. It is imperative to acknowledge the bidirectional relationship between emotions and behavior in the context of operant conditioning. Emotions not only serve as powerful reinforcers or punishers but also contribute to the acquisition of new behaviors and the extinction of existing ones. For instance, the experience of joy following a successful task completion can reinforce the likelihood of repeating the behavior, while the fear of failure can act as a powerful deterrent. Recognizing the nuanced influence of emotions on behavior is crucial for designing effective behavioral modification strategies. Integrating emotional regulation techniques, such as mindfulness practices and cognitive reappraisal, into behavior modification interventions holds promise for enhancing treatment outcomes.

8. Social Contexts and Behavioral Adaptations:

In the field of behavioral psychology, the influence of social contexts on individual behavioral adaptations is a topic of profound importance and complexity. Social environments play a critical role in shaping and molding human behavior, often serving as powerful determinants of an individual's actions and responses. Through social interactions, individuals exhibit a wide range of behavioral adaptations that are acutely tuned to the dynamics of their immediate social milieu. Understanding the mechanisms through which social contexts impact behavioral adaptations provides invaluable insights into the complexities of human behavior.

One key aspect of social contexts influencing behavioral adaptations lies in the power of social norms and expectations. These societal standards and unwritten rules serve as both explicit and implicit guides for individual behavior within a given community or group. The adherence to social norms, or conversely, the deviation from them, can significantly shape an individual's behavioral repertoire. As such, individuals often demonstrate remarkable adaptive abilities to conform or adjust their behavior according to the prevailing social norms, thereby exhibiting a high degree of malleability in response to social pressures.

The concept of social modeling, proposed by renowned psychologist Albert Bandura, elucidates how individuals acquire new behaviors through observation and imitation of others within their social milieu. By observing and mimicking the actions of role models or peers, individuals undergo behavioral adaptations that are heavily influenced by their social environment. This process not only facilitates the assimilation of new behavioral patterns but also underscores the impact of social context in driving behavioral change.

An individual's social network and interpersonal relationships significantly contribute to shaping their behavioral adaptations. The quality and nature of social connections, including family dynamics, friendships, and professional relationships, exert profound influences on an individual's behavior. Social support systems, for instance, have been shown to foster positive behavioral adaptations, while social isolation or adversarial relationships may lead to maladaptive behaviors. The dynamic interplay between an individual's social affiliations and their resulting behavioral adaptations underscores the relationship between social contexts and human behavior.

Additionally, cultural influences within social contexts are pivotal in shaping behavioral adaptations across diverse populations. Cultural norms, traditions, and values mold the behavioral expressions of individuals within a specific cultural milieu. Understanding the nuanced interplay between culture and behavior provides crucial insights into the adaptive behaviors observed within different cultural groups, emphasizing the significance of social contexts in driving behavioral diversity.

The Definition of Reinforcement - Positive and Negative

1. Historical Perspectives on Reinforcement Theory:

The historical roots of reinforcement theory stretch back to the early 20th century with the pioneering work of researchers such as Edward Thorndike and B.F. Skinner. Thorndike's influential 'law of effect' proposed that behaviors followed by favorable outcomes are more likely to be repeated, while those followed by unfavorable outcomes are less likely to be repeated. This laid the groundwork for understanding the principles of reinforcement and its role in shaping behavior.

Building on Thorndike's work, B.F. Skinner further elaborated on the concept of reinforcement, distinguishing between positive and negative reinforcement. His development of the operant conditioning chamber, or 'Skinner box', allowed for controlled studies on the effects of reinforcement on behavior. These foundational experiments provided empirical support for the principles of reinforcement and led to the development of modern behavioral theories.

The evolution of reinforcement theory also saw the integration of cognitive perspectives, with researchers like Albert Bandura emphasizing the role of cognitive processes in learning through reinforcement. Bandura's social learning theory expanded the understanding of reinforcement beyond direct conditioning, illustrating the impact of observational learning and modeling in reinforcing behaviors.

The application of reinforcement principles extended beyond academic research to real-world settings, such as education, clinical psychology, and organizational behavior management. The implications of reinforcement theory have had a profound influence on diverse fields, enhancing our comprehension of human behavior and the mechanisms of behavioral change.

Over time, the theoretical underpinnings of reinforcement have been refined and expanded, incorporating interdisciplinary insights from neuroscience, psychology, and behavioral economics. Contemporary perspectives continue to explore the complexities of reinforcement processes, including the nuanced interactions between individual differences, cultural factors, and environmental influences.

2. Mechanisms and Applications of Positive Reinforcement:

Positive reinforcement is a powerful tool in shaping behavior, encompassing a wide array of mechanisms and applications that have profound implications in various domains. At its core, positive reinforcement involves the presentation of a desirable stimulus following a behavior, leading to an increased likelihood of the behavior's recurrence. One of the fundamental mechanisms underlying positive reinforcement is the concept of operant conditioning, in which the consequences of an action influence the likelihood of its repetition. This form of conditioning fosters learning through the association of behaviors with positive outcomes.

In practical terms, positive reinforcement can be applied across diverse settings, including education, therapy, and organizational management. In educational contexts, educators leverage positive reinforcement to motivate students, cultivate desired behaviors, and facilitate the learning process. By offering praise, rewards, or privileges for exemplary performance or adherence to classroom rules, teachers can create a positive and supportive learning environment while encouraging academic engagement and achievement.

Positive reinforcement plays a pivotal role in therapeutic interventions, particularly in behavioral therapies. Behavioral therapists utilize positive reinforcement to encourage adaptive behaviors and discourage maladaptive ones, thereby contributing to the improvement of mental health conditions and the enhancement of overall well-being. The application of positive reinforcement in therapeutic settings extends to diverse populations, from children with developmental disorders to individuals coping with addiction or anxiety.

In addition to education and therapy, positive reinforcement strategies are also instrumental in organizational management. Leaders can employ positive reinforcement techniques to motivate employees, strengthen workplace morale, and shape a positive corporate culture. By recognizing and rewarding exceptional performance, fostering a supportive work environment, and providing opportunities for professional growth, organizations can enhance employee satisfaction, productivity, and retention.

It is crucial to acknowledge the ethical considerations and potential limitations associated with the use of positive reinforcement. While effectively shaping behavior, overreliance on positive reinforcement alone may raise concerns about intrinsic motivation and autonomy. Therefore, careful implementation and consideration of individual differences are essential when applying positive reinforcement techniques, ensuring a balanced approach to behavior modification.

3. Positive vs. Negative Reinforcement:

Positive reinforcement involves the presentation of a desirable stimulus following a behavior, with the aim of increasing the likelihood of that behavior being repeated in the future. In contrast, negative reinforcement entails the removal or avoidance of an aversive stimulus upon the occurrence of a specific behavior, thereby reinforcing the likelihood of that behavior recurring. Despite their divergent mechanisms, both positive and negative reinforcement serve as potent tools for shaping behavior.

One significant distinction lies in the nature of the stimuli involved. Positive reinforcement introduces a favorable consequence to bolster a behavior, such as offering praise for completing a task or providing a treat for desired actions from a pet. On the other hand, negative reinforcement revolves around the removal of an unpleasant stimulus after the execution of a targeted behavior, exemplified by turning off a loud alarm after taking a prescribed action or avoiding an uncomfortable situation through specific behavior. Understanding this dissimilarity is crucial in developing interventions tailored to specific behavioral patterns.

The timing and manner of application differ for positive and negative reinforcement. Positive reinforcement typically necessitates prompt delivery of the reinforcing stimulus following the desired behavior to establish the association effectively. Conversely, negative reinforcement requires the termination of the aversive stimulus once the targeted behavior occurs. This timing discrepancy underscores the necessity for a nuanced approach when implementing reinforcement strategies.

Another key aspect to consider is the potential impact on individual motivation and emotional response. While positive reinforcement often fosters feelings of encouragement, satisfaction, and fulfillment, negative reinforcement may lead to relief from anxiety, stress, or discomfort. Recognizing the psychological implications of each form of reinforcement is vital in gauging their efficacy and ethical considerations in behavioral interventions.

Understanding the differentiation between positive and negative reinforcement is central to leveraging operant conditioning principles for behavior modification. It enables us to design tailored reinforcement plans that align with specific behaviors and individuals' needs, maximizing the effectiveness of interventions. By appreciating the nuanced distinctions and applications of positive and negative reinforcement, one can harness these mechanisms to facilitate positive behavioral changes and optimize learning outcomes.

4. Empirical Studies Supporting Reinforcement Principles:

Empirical research provides scientific evidence for the effectiveness of different reinforcement strategies and helps us understand the mechanisms underlying behavior modification. Countless experimental studies have explored the impact of reinforcement on various behaviors, shedding light on its diverse applications across different settings. These studies often employ rigorous methodologies, including controlled experiments, observational analyses, and systematic manipulation of variables to investigate how reinforcement influences behavior.

One impactful area of empirical research focuses on the use of positive reinforcement in education. Numerous studies have demonstrated the effectiveness of employing positive reinforcement techniques to enhance learning outcomes in both academic and behavioral domains. By systematically reinforcing desired behaviors with rewards such as praise, privileges, or tangible incentives, educators have been able to positively shape student behaviors and encourage active engagement in the learning process. These findings underscore the practical value of positive reinforcement in educational settings and highlight its potential to foster a conducive learning environment.

empirical investigations have delved into the implications of reinforcement schedules on behavior. Through meticulously designed studies involving reinforcement schedules, researchers have elucidated the differential effects of various reinforcement contingencies, including fixed ratio, variable ratio, fixed interval, and variable interval schedules. These studies have not only provided insights into the predictability and persistence of behavior under different reinforcement schedules but have also contributed to the development of comprehensive theories regarding schedule-induced behaviors and choice behavior.

Additionally, empirical studies have examined the utilization of reinforcement techniques in clinical and therapeutic contexts. Research in this area has offered compelling evidence for the efficacy of reinforcement-based interventions in addressing a wide range of behavioral issues, including phobias, addictions, and developmental disorders. By systematically reinforcing adaptive or desired behaviors while extinguishing maladaptive ones, clinicians and therapists have achieved significant improvements in patients' behavior and emotional well-being, thereby underscoring the clinical relevance and effectiveness of reinforcement principles.

5. Reinforcement Schedules:

Reinforcement schedules refer to the specific patterns or sequences by which reinforcements are delivered following particular behaviors. These schedules can vary based on the timing and frequency of reinforcements, ultimately shaping the durability and strength of the learned behaviors. There are several types of reinforcement schedules, each exerting distinct effects on behavior.

One of the most fundamental reinforcement schedules is the continuous reinforcement schedule, wherein the desired behavior is reinforced every time it occurs. This schedule is exceptionally effective in initially establishing and strengthening the desired behavior. However, it may not always be feasible or practical for long-term maintenance of behavior due to resource constraints or potential over-reliance on continuous reinforcement.

In contrast, intermittent reinforcement schedules involve reinforcing the desired behavior only occasionally. These schedules can take various forms, such as fixed ratio, variable ratio, fixed interval, and variable interval schedules. Each type of schedule has unique characteristics that influence behavior in different ways. For instance, fixed ratio schedules reinforce behavior after a specific number of responses, while variable interval schedules reinforce behavior after unpredictable time intervals.

The choice of the reinforcement schedule holds substantial significance, as it directly impacts the rate of response, resistance to extinction, and overall behavioral consistency. The manipulation of reinforcement schedules is prevalent in various real-world settings, including education, parenting, and organizational management.

Understanding the effects of different reinforcement schedules is essential for practitioners and educators seeking to effectively shape and maintain desired behaviors. Moreover, the knowledge of reinforcement schedules serves as a valuable tool for addressing maladaptive behaviors and promoting positive change. By strategically applying reinforcement schedules, individuals can create sustainable behavior change and cultivate environments conducive to learning and growth.

As advancements in behavioral research continue to unfold, further exploration into the complexities of reinforcement schedules and their nuanced effects on behavior is imperative. Increased comprehension of these dynamics offers vast potential for refining interventions, enhancing instructional methods, and optimizing behavioral management strategies across diverse domains.

6. Challenges and Misconceptions in Reinforcement Application:

The effective application of reinforcement methods in behavior modification encounters various challenges and misconceptions that warrant careful consideration. One notable challenge lies in the complexity of individual behaviors as they interact with diverse environmental factors. It can be difficult to accurately predict behavioral responses and identify suitable reinforcements for each unique scenario. Furthermore, misconceptions surrounding reinforcement techniques may arise due to misinterpretations or oversimplifications of behavioral theories. This can lead to misguided attempts at modifying behavior without achieving desired outcomes. Additionally, ethical considerations in reinforcement application present a significant challenge, as ensuring the well-being and autonomy of individuals is paramount. Avoiding coercion and respecting personal boundaries while implementing reinforcement strategies requires thoughtful navigation of ethical dilemmas. Another challenge is the potential for unintended consequences when employing reinforcement. While the intended behavior may be reinforced, there is a risk of inadvertently reinforcing undesirable behaviors. This underscores the importance of precise reinforcement delivery and continuous monitoring to mitigate such occurrences. Inaccurate or inconsistent reinforcement may result in the reinforcement of unintended behaviors, thereby hindering the overall effectiveness of the intervention. Moreover, the sustainability and long-term maintenance of reinforced behaviors pose a considerable challenge. Ensuring that the effects of reinforcement endure beyond the immediate intervention period demands strategic planning and comprehensive follow-up measures. An additional challenge arises from the need to adapt reinforcement strategies to accommodate individual differences and contextual variations, acknowledging that what works for one person may not be effective for another. Addressing misconceptions in reinforcement application involves dispelling myths and elucidating the nuanced principles underlying operant conditioning. Common misconceptions, such as equating reinforcement solely with rewards or overlooking the intricacies of negative reinforcement, require clarification to foster a more accurate understanding of these concepts. Additionally, overcoming the misconception that reinforcement is exclusively applicable in controlled experimental settings is essential. Real-world application of reinforcement techniques necessitates an awareness of the dynamic and multifaceted nature of behavior-environment interactions. To navigate these challenges and misconceptions, practitioners should engage in ongoing education and training, drawing on evidence-based practices and case studies to enhance their proficiency in reinforcement application.

Mechanisms of Punishment - Classification and Strategies

1. Punishment within Operant Conditioning Framework:

Punishment within the context of operant conditioning serves as a critical mechanism for modifying behavior. Unlike reinforcement, which aims to strengthen and increase the likelihood of specific behaviors, punishment encompasses the application of aversive consequences to decrease or suppress undesirable actions or responses. Inherent to this concept is the idea that following an unwanted behavior, the introduction of an adverse outcome or removal of a positive stimulus acts to deter the recurrence of that behavior in the future. This process aligns with the principles of operant conditioning, where behavior is shaped by its consequences.

In applying punishment, it is essential to recognize that the effectiveness of this technique is contingent on various factors, including the timing, consistency, and intensity of the aversive stimuli. Moreover, understanding the distinction between punishment and negative reinforcement is crucial. While punishment seeks to dissuade certain behaviors through the imposition of unfavorable outcomes, negative reinforcement operates by removing or avoiding adverse stimuli upon the manifestation of desired conduct, thereby strengthening the probability of such behavior reoccurring.

Within the operant conditioning framework, two primary categories of punishment exist: positive and negative. Positive punishment entails the administration of an unpleasant stimulus following an unwanted behavior, whereas negative punishment involves the removal of a desirable stimulus subsequent to the same undesired action. Through these mechanisms, individuals and organisms learn to associate specific behaviors with unfavorable ramifications, ultimately adjusting their behavioral repertoire to mitigate such consequences.

It is important to highlight that the efficacy of punishment is intrinsically tied to the individual's cognitive and emotional processing. Cognitive and affective factors influence how the recipient interprets and responds to punitive measures. Additionally, ethical considerations play a pivotal role in determining the appropriateness of implementing punishment in behavioral modification practices. As such, careful attention must be given to the potential psychological impact of employing punitive measures, particularly considering the potential implications for mental well-being and overall welfare.

Recognizing the limitations and potential drawbacks of punishment within the operant conditioning paradigm is essential. While punishment may initially lead to a reduction in undesired behaviors, there is a risk of unintended side effects, such as increased anxiety, resistance, or the development of alternate maladaptive behaviors as coping mechanisms. Therefore, a comprehensive understanding of punishment within the operant conditioning framework necessitates an exploration of its nuanced implications and strategic application to ensure ethical and pragmatic utilization for behavioral modification.

2. The Distinction Between Punishment and Reinforcement:

Reinforcement involves the process of strengthening a specific behavior by providing a consequence in response to that behavior. This consequence can be either positive, involving the addition of a rewarding stimulus, or negative, entailing the removal of an aversive stimulus. On the other hand, punishment aims to decrease the likelihood of a behavior recurring by introducing an aversive consequence following the behavior.

One key differentiator between punishment and reinforcement lies in their underlying purpose. Reinforcement seeks to encourage and promote a desired behavior, whereas punishment is implemented to discourage and reduce the occurrence of an undesired behavior. It is essential for practitioners of operant conditioning to grasp this fundamental dissimilarity, as misapplication or confusion between the two can significantly impact behavioral outcomes.

Reinforcement and punishment differ in terms of the specific consequences they produce. Reinforcement results in the strengthening or enhancement of a behavior, making it more likely to occur in the future. Conversely, punishment leads to the weakening or suppression of a behavior, reducing its future likelihood. Understanding these distinct outcomes is imperative when selecting the appropriate approach to modify behavior effectively.

Another critical factor in differentiating punishment from reinforcement relates to the emotional and psychological impact on the individual. Reinforcement, particularly positive reinforcement, often generates feelings of reward, satisfaction, and motivation, reinforcing the individual's association with the desired behavior. In contrast, punishment introduces aversive consequences that may induce anxiety, fear, or distress, potentially leading to negative psychological associations with the targeted behavior.

The timing and consistency of application also distinguish punishment from reinforcement. Reinforcement must be timely and consistent to effectively reinforce the desired behavior. In contrast, punishment necessitates prompt and consistent administration but should also be applied sparingly and judiciously to avoid unintended side effects, such as increased aggression or learned helplessness.

3. Types of Punishment - Positive and Negative:

In the context of operant conditioning, punishment serves as a critical tool for modifying behavior through the application of aversive consequences. Positive punishment involves the administration of an unfavorable stimulus following a behavior in order to decrease the likelihood of that behavior recurring in the future. On the other hand, negative punishment entails the removal of a desirable stimulus in response to a behavior, with the goal of reducing the occurrence of that behavior in subsequent situations. Understanding the distinction between these two forms of punishment is fundamental in designing effective behavior modification strategies. Positive punishment relies on the presentation of something undesirable to deter the undesired behavior, while negative punishment focuses on taking away something desirable to achieve the same objective. The consequences associated with each type of punishment play a crucial role in shaping the individual's behavioral responses. Both positive and negative punishment have implications for the emotional and cognitive processes of the individuals subjected to them. The psychological impact of experiencing either form of punishment can influence the individual's attitude towards the specific behavior and even towards the individual administering the punishment. It is important to consider the potential side effects and ethical implications of utilizing punishment in behavior modification. When implementing positive punishment, careful consideration must be given to the nature of the aversive stimulus to ensure that it is appropriate and proportional to the behavior being targeted. Likewise, in the case of negative punishment, removing a desired stimulus should effectively communicate the consequence of the behavior without causing unnecessary distress

4. The Aversive Stimulus:

An aversive stimulus, within the context of operant conditioning, refers to a stimuli that an organism will consistently work to avoid. It involves the presentation or occurrence of something displeasurable, which results in a decrease in the behavior that precedes it. A fundamental aspect of understanding the aversive stimulus lies in comprehending its impact on behavior and learning processes. When individuals experience an aversive stimulus following a specific behavior, they are inclined to modify their actions to avoid encountering it in the future. Aversive stimuli can take various forms, ranging from physical discomfort to emotional distress. For example, in a controlled experimental setting, an aversive stimulus might involve mild electric shocks, loud noises, or unpleasant odors. In real-world scenarios, aversive stimuli could encompass reprimands, criticisms, or social exclusion. The intensity and duration of these aversive stimuli can significantly influence their impact on behavior.

5. Variables Influencing the Efficacy of Punishment:

The efficacy of punishment in behavioral modification is influenced by a myriad of variables that warrant careful consideration. One pivotal factor is the timing of the punishment relative to the undesirable behavior. Research has consistently shown that immediate, rather than delayed, punishment is more effective in suppressing the targeted behavior. This underscores the importance of timely and consistent application of punishment within the operant conditioning framework.

The intensity of the punitive stimulus plays a critical role in determining its effectiveness. While it is essential to administer an aversive stimulus with sufficient impact to deter the unwanted behavior, excessive intensity may lead to adverse consequences such as heightened fear or anxiety. Therefore, striking a balance in the intensity of punishment is crucial in achieving the desired behavioral change.

Another variable that significantly influences the efficacy of punishment is its consistency. Consistent application of punishment following the undesired behavior reinforces the association between the behavior and the aversive consequences, thereby facilitating the extinction of the behavior over time. Inconsistent or sporadic punishment, on the other hand, may lead to confusion and impede the desired outcomes.

The nature of the punished behavior and the individual differences among subjects also need to be taken into account when assessing the efficacy of punishment. Certain behaviors may be more resistant to punishment due to their inherent reinforcing qualities or the individual's predisposition. Understanding these nuances is essential for tailoring punishment strategies to effectively address specific behavioral issues.

Additionally, the environment in which the punishment is administered can impact its efficacy. Factors such as the presence of alternative reinforcement sources, social dynamics, and the overall context in which the behavior occurs can influence how punishment is perceived and its subsequent impact on behavior modification.

6. Ethical Considerations in the Application of Punishment:

The application of punishment in behavioral modification raises significant ethical considerations that must be carefully addressed. One fundamental ethical concern pertains to the potential for harm when administering punishment. While punishment may be intended to deter undesirable behaviors, its implementation can lead to adverse emotional and psychological effects on the individual being subjected to the aversive stimulus. This is particularly relevant when considering the use of physical or emotional punishment, as they can result in lasting trauma and damage to the individual's well-being.

Additionally, there is a critical ethical issue regarding the degree of control and consent in the application of punishment. In many settings, individuals may not have the autonomy or voice to object to the punitive measures imposed upon them. This lack of agency raises questions about the fairness and justice of employing punishment as a means of behavior modification. Moreover, the power dynamics involved in administering punishment demand careful consideration to ensure that it is not exercised arbitrarily or abusively.

Ethical dilemmas emerge when addressing the long-term implications of punishment. While punishment may suppress unwanted behaviors in the short term, its enduring impact on the individual's mental and emotional state, as well as their relationship with the enforcer, needs thorough examination. There is a need to assess whether punitive measures foster a healthy and supportive environment conducive to sustainable behavioral change without compromising the individual's dignity and autonomy.

Another profound ethical matter centers on the alternatives to punishment within the context of behavioral modification. It is essential to explore and prioritize positive reinforcement and non-coercive strategies to elicit desirable behaviors. Emphasizing the promotion of constructive behaviors rather than relying solely on punitive measures aligns with the ethical principle of fostering growth and development without resorting to punitive tactics.

7. Strategies for Implementing Effective Punishment:

The successful implementation of punishment as a behavioral modification strategy necessitates a judicious approach that considers the individualized nature of behavior and the significance of ethical considerations. Establishing effective strategies for punishment entails a comprehensive understanding of the circumstances under which punishment is being applied, as well as the potential impact it may have on the individual or subject in question. When considering the implementation of punishment, it is crucial to first identify the specific behavior that requires modification. Clear and specific delineation of the targeted behavior ensures that the application of punishment remains focused and purposeful. Moreover, the importance of consistency cannot be overstated. Consistency in the application of punishment involves ensuring that undesired behaviors are consistently met with the predetermined consequences, thereby reinforcing the cause-and-effect relationship between the behavior and its repercussions. Additionally, setting clear expectations and transparently communicating the consequences of behaviors aids in fostering an environment where individuals comprehend the implications of their actions. It is imperative to establish a tangible system of rewards and recognition for positive behavior alongside the punitive measures, promoting a balanced approach toward behavioral modification. Furthermore, tailoring the punishment to be commensurate with the infraction committed is pivotal. The severity and duration of the punitive measures should correlate directly with the degree of the transgression, thereby aligning the consequences with the behavior exhibited. In addressing the effectiveness of punishment, consideration must also be given to the timeliness of its administration. Promptly meting out the consequence following the occurrence of the undesired behavior reinforces the association between the two, enhancing the potential for behavioral adjustment. Equally important is the need for continuous monitoring of the repercussions of punishment. Regular evaluation of the impact of punitive measures on the individual's behavior serves to gauge the efficacy of the strategy and determine necessary adjustments. This involves vigilance in observing not only short-term changes in behavior but also the long-term effects that may manifest over time. Ultimately, adopting a multifaceted approach that combines diligent observation, consistent application, ethical consciousness, and personalized calibration is instrumental in implementing effective punishment as a means of behavioral modification.

8. Measuring the Impact - Short-Term vs. Long-Term Effects:

Understanding the short-term and long-term effects of implementing punitive measures is crucial for gaining insight into their overall efficacy. Short-term effects often manifest immediately following the administration of punishment. These can include a temporary decrease in the frequency of the targeted behavior, or an initial display of avoidance responses. However, it is essential to delve deeper and consider the potential resurgence of the behavior once the punitive measures are removed. This phenomenon highlights the importance of assessing the long-term effects of punishment. Long-term effects encompass the sustained impact of punitive interventions on behavior over extended periods. It is essential to recognize that the repercussions of punishment can extend beyond the immediate suppression of behavior. For instance, individuals subjected to punitive measures may experience heightened levels of stress and anxiety, which can have enduring effects on their emotional well-being and relationship with the punisher. Moreover, the long-term effectiveness of punishment in altering behavior necessitates analysis from multiple perspectives, including its influence on the individual's motivation, resilience, and overall psychological state. Evaluating the long-term consequences also involves examining potential implications for the individual's perception of authority figures, the learning environment, and their intrinsic motivation. Considering these dynamics, researchers and practitioners must adopt a meticulous approach toward assessing the lasting impact of punishment, taking into account individual differences, situational factors, and the ethical considerations inherent in the application of punitive strategies. Employing robust assessment tools, such as longitudinal studies, behavioral observations, and self-report measures, can provide valuable insights into the enduring ramifications of employing punishment in behavior modification programs. Furthermore, capturing the long-term effects of punishment necessitates a nuanced understanding of behavior change processes, encompassing not only observable actions but also cognitive and emotional facets.

Extinction in Behavioral Contexts

1. Historical Foundations of Extinction in Psychology:

Extinction, as a concept within the field of psychology, has deep historical roots that have significantly influenced its understanding and application in behavioral contexts. The origins of extinction can be traced back to the work of Ivan Pavlov, whose groundbreaking research on classical conditioning laid the groundwork for subsequent explorations of learning and behavior. It was through Pavlov's experiments with dogs that the phenomenon of extinction began to emerge as a pivotal component of behavioral modification. By systematically presenting conditioned stimuli without the subsequent unconditioned stimulus, Pavlov observed a gradual decrease in the conditioned response, a process he termed 'extinction.' This early work laid the foundation for the systematic study of extinction and its implications for behaviorism. Beyond Pavlov, eminent figures such as B.F. Skinner further advanced the understanding of extinction within the broader framework of operant conditioning. Skinner's influential experiments with reinforcement schedules and the extinguishing of previously reinforced behaviors contributed significantly to the evolution of extinction theory. Moreover, the historical progression of extinction within psychology reflects shifts in theoretical paradigms and methodologies, revealing the enduring relevance of this concept in shaping our understanding of human and animal behavior. As psychological perspectives evolved, so too did the conceptualization of extinction, leading to nuanced interpretations that integrated cognitive and emotional factors into the extinction process. The historical foundations of extinction in psychology not only shed light on its empirical underpinnings but also underscore its enduring importance in contemporary research and applied settings.

2. Theoretical Frameworks Underlying Extinction:

Extinction, as a behavioral process, is anchored in various theoretical frameworks that have contributed to our understanding of how behaviors cease to manifest in response to specific environmental cues or stimuli. One prominent theoretical framework is rooted in the principles of operant conditioning, where the concept of extinction underscores the absence of reinforcement following the occurrence of a previously reinforced behavior. According to this framework, the underlying mechanism of extinction centers on the removal of the reinforcing consequence, leading to a reduction in the frequency and strength of the targeted behavior. This causal relationship between the removal of reinforcement and the subsequent decline of the behavior forms the basis of the operant conditioning perspective on extinction. Another theoretical framework originates from the field of cognitive psychology, where the cognitive processes involved in extinction phenomena are explored. Cognitive theories posit that extinction involves a reevaluation of the learned associations between stimuli and responses, leading to the gradual weakening or erasure of the previously acquired behavioral patterns. These theories emphasize the role of mental representations, perception, and memory processes in the extinction of behaviors and elucidate the cognitive restructuring that occurs during the extinction process. Moreover, evolutionary theories provide an additional perspective on extinction by situating it within the broader context of adaptive behavior. From an evolutionary standpoint, extinction is construed as an adaptive mechanism that allows organisms to recalibrate their behavioral repertoires in response to changes in the environment. This framework emphasizes the adaptive value of extinguishing obsolete behaviors and highlights the evolutionary benefits associated with the ability to cease unproductive or maladaptive behaviors. Furthermore, neuroscientific approaches to extinction elucidate the neural substrates and processes involved in the extinction of behaviors. They delve into the neurobiological underpinnings of extinction, emphasizing the role of neural plasticity, synaptic modifications, and neurotransmitter systems in mediating the extinction process. Insights from neuroscience offer a comprehensive understanding of the neural mechanisms that underlie the encoding, retrieval, and extinction of learned behaviors, shedding light on the interplay between brain structures and behavioral outcomes.

3. Extinction vs. Punishment - Conceptual Clarifications:

Extinction refers to the gradual weakening and eventual suppression of a previously reinforced behavior due to the absence of reinforcing consequences. In contrast, punishment involves the presentation of aversive consequences following a behavior, leading to a decrease in the frequency or likelihood of that behavior recurring. One fundamental difference lies in the nature of the effects on behavior: while extinction results in the behavior becoming less frequent and eventually ceasing, punishment aims to actively reduce the occurrence of the targeted behavior through the application of punitive measures. Furthermore, the mechanisms underlying extinction and punishment diverge in terms of their impact on the individual's learning and motivation. Extinction primarily focuses on the removal of reinforcement, thereby altering the individual's expectation of obtaining desirable outcomes, whereas punishment introduces an element of discomfort or aversion associated with the behavior, influencing the individual's response through negative associations. It is essential to recognize that the distinction between extinction and punishment extends beyond their immediate outcomes to encompass the broader ethical and practical considerations in behavioral interventions. When implementing extinction procedures, practitioners must carefully navigate the potential ethical implications of withholding reinforcement, ensuring that alternative methods are employed to address the targeted behavior effectively. Conversely, the application of punishment necessitates a thorough evaluation of its appropriateness and potential unintended consequences, emphasizing the need for responsible and informed decision-making.

4. The Process of Extinction:

Extinction involves the gradual weakening and eventual suppression of a previously reinforced behavior as a result of its non-reinforcement. Understanding the mechanisms and stages of extinction is pivotal for practitioners and researchers alike. The process of extinction encompasses several interconnected mechanisms that contribute to its efficacy. Firstly, it involves the disruption of the established contingency between the behavior and its reinforcing consequence. This disrupts the learned association, leading to a decline in the frequency and strength of the targeted behavior. Additionally, extinction entails an element of inhibitory learning, wherein individuals learn that the once-reinforcing stimulus no longer holds its previous value. As a result, the behavior decreases as the individual ceases to expect the reinforcing consequence. Furthermore, the process of extinction operates within a broader context of response generalization, where the absence of reinforcement extends to similar behaviors, contributing to their decline as well. These mechanisms collectively underpin the complex process of extinction. The process of extinction unfolds in distinct stages, each with its characteristic features. Initially, when reinforcement ceases, there is a temporary increase in the frequency and intensity of the behavior. This phenomenon, referred to as an extinction burst, is an expected occurrence as the individual tests the exhaustiveness of the reinforcement schedule before gradually decreasing the behavior.

Subsequently, the behavior enters a phase of variability, displaying fluctuations in frequency and intensity as the individual seeks alternative responses to obtain reinforcement. It is imperative for practitioners to be cognizant of this phase to effectively manage and address the behavior undergoing extinction. Following the variability stage, there is a subsequent decline in the frequency of the behavior until it reaches a stable state of minimal occurrence.

5. Factors Influencing the Efficacy of Extinction Procedures:

Extinction procedures, while powerful in their potential to modify behavior, are influenced by a myriad of factors that can significantly impact their efficacy. One key factor influencing the efficacy of extinction procedures is the initial strength of the reinforced behavior. Behaviors that have been consistently reinforced over time, especially those with a high reinforcement schedule, may prove more resistant to extinction, requiring prolonged and consistent implementation of extinction procedures. Furthermore, the timing and consistency of implementing extinction procedures play a crucial role. Inconsistent or intermittent application of extinction can lead to the occasional re-emergence of the extinguished behavior, known as spontaneous recovery. Additionally, the context in which extinction occurs is pivotal. Environmental cues and situational factors can impact the generalization of extinction effects, emphasizing the importance of conducting extinction in varied contexts to promote broad behavioral change. Another critical consideration is the presence of alternative sources of reinforcement. If alternative sources of reinforcement are readily available, the extinction of a specific behavior may be impeded. Additionally, individual differences in learning history, motivation, and cognitive processes can influence the response to extinction procedures. These individual variations necessitate tailored approaches and careful consideration of the unique characteristics of the learner. The emotional and affective state of the organism also plays a role in the efficacy of extinction, as heightened emotional arousal can impact the extinction process. Factors such as fear and anxiety may complicate the extinction of certain behaviors, highlighting the need for comprehensive assessment and management of emotional responses during extinction procedures. Finally, the duration and intensity of extinction procedures must be carefully deliberated. While prolonged exposure to extinction trials may yield favorable outcomes, excessively lengthy procedures can induce frustration and extinction-induced aggression. A balanced approach, informed by an understanding of these multifaceted factors, is essential for optimizing the efficacy of extinction procedures.

6. Challenges and Misconceptions in Implementing Extinction:

Implementing extinction strategies in behavioral contexts presents a myriad of challenges and misconceptions that necessitate careful consideration. One of the primary challenges lies in the potential resurgence of previously extinguished behavior, especially when the extinction procedure is not consistently maintained. This phenomenon underscores the critical need for vigilance and adherence to the extinction protocol to prevent the reemergence of undesired behaviors. Furthermore, the temporal persistence of extinction effects poses a challenge, as individuals or organisms may exhibit temporary suppression of behavior rather than permanent cessation. This transient reduction in behavior can lead to misconceptions about the effectiveness of extinction, emphasizing the importance of sustained implementation and monitoring. Misunderstandings surrounding the definition and application of extinction can also impede its successful implementation. Clear communication and education are imperative in dispelling misconceptions and ensuring that the extinction process is correctly understood and executed. Additionally, ethical considerations and potential aversive effects associated with extinction techniques present ethical and practical challenges. Balancing the ethical use of extinction with the desired behavioral outcomes requires thorough assessment and consideration of potential implications on the well-being of the subject. Practical constraints, such as resource limitations and environmental factors, further compound the challenges in implementing extinction procedures effectively. Understanding these challenges and misconceptions is crucial for practitioners and researchers in the field of behavioral modification. Addressing these issues through ongoing training, supervision, and research can enhance the successful application of extinction strategies and contribute to the advancement of behavioral interventions. By actively acknowledging these challenges, professionals can mitigate potential pitfalls and optimize the outcomes of extinction-based approaches within diverse behavioral contexts.

7. The Integration of Extinction with Reinforcement Strategies:

While extinction involves the removal of reinforcement following a target behavior, reinforcement strategies focus on increasing the likelihood of a behavior recurring through the application of positive or negative reinforcements. By understanding the nuances of integrating extinction with reinforcement strategies, practitioners can effectively design interventions to address maladaptive behaviors across various settings.

One key consideration in integrating extinction with reinforcement strategies is the careful assessment of target behaviors and their antecedents. Identifying the specific triggers and environmental cues that elicit the undesired behavior is essential for crafting an effective intervention plan. Once these antecedents are identified, reinforcement strategies can be employed to promote alternative, adaptive behaviors. Simultaneously, extinction procedures can be implemented to systematically reduce the frequency of the maladaptive behavior by withholding the reinforcing consequences that previously maintained it.

Successful integration requires a nuanced understanding of the potential side effects and challenges associated with extinction procedures. For instance, practitioners must remain attentive to the possibility of an initial increase in the frequency or intensity of the targeted behavior—often referred to as an extinction burst—before seeing a decrease in the behavior. Additionally, the occurrence of spontaneous recovery, where the previously extinguished behavior resurfaces after a period of non-reinforcement, necessitates strategic planning to prevent relapse.

The timing and consistency of reinforcement delivery are vital components of integrating extinction with reinforcement strategies. Balancing the gradual fading of reinforcement for the undesired behavior while consistently reinforcing the desired alternative behavior is a delicate process. This necessitates precise planning and ongoing evaluation to ensure that the rate and schedule of reinforcement align with the goals of the intervention.

Equally important is the ethical implementation of extinction within the framework of reinforcement strategies. Practitioners must prioritize the welfare and rights of the individuals undergoing behavior modification and ensure that extinction procedures are utilized with care and expertise. When implemented ethically and effectively, the integration of extinction with reinforcement strategies can contribute significantly to the long-term success of behavior modification interventions and foster lasting behavioral change.

EXAMPLES AND ILLUSTRATIONS

Real-World Examples of Operant Conditioning

Operant conditioning is interwoven into numerous facets of everyday life. Consider the widespread use of reward systems in the workplace—employees may receive bonuses or other incentives for meeting performance targets, illustrating the application of positive reinforcement. Conversely, punitive measures such as fines for traffic violations exemplify the implementation of punishment to decrease unwanted behaviors. Within the field of consumer behavior, loyalty programs offered by businesses reflect the utilization of reinforcement strategies to shape purchasing habits. Moreover, the prevalence of smartphone addiction underscores the unintended consequences of intermittent reinforcement schedules, leading individuals to compulsively check their devices. The impact of social media platforms on behavior, with likes and comments serving as reinforcing stimuli, further highlights the omnipresence of operant conditioning in contemporary society. In the field of sports, coaches employ reinforcement techniques to enhance athletes' skills and motivation, ultimately influencing performance outcomes. Furthermore, the design of educational software often incorporates operant conditioning principles, utilizing interactive feedback and rewards to facilitate learning.

Operant Conditioning in Educational Settings

Educators and psychologists have long recognized the potential of operant conditioning in shaping and modifying learning behaviors among students. When discussing operant conditioning in educational settings, one important application is related to behavior management. By implementing reinforcement strategies, educators can encourage positive behavior and discourage negative conduct in the classroom. Through the use of positive reinforcement such as praise, rewards, or privileges, teachers can reinforce desirable behaviors, thereby increasing the likelihood of their recurrence. Negative reinforcement, involving the removal of aversive stimuli following desired behavior, can also contribute to reinforcing positive conduct among students.

The concept of shaping behavior through successive approximations proves to be valuable in educational contexts. Utilizing this technique, educators can gradually guide students toward exhibiting the desired behavior by reinforcing small steps towards the ultimate goal. This approach is particularly effective in teaching complex skills or when working with students who may initially struggle with certain tasks.

Considering the role of punishment, it is essential to exercise caution in educational settings. While punishment can be used to deter undesirable behaviors, it needs to be implemented judiciously and in adherence to ethical considerations. Uncontrolled use of punishment may lead to adverse emotional or psychological effects on students and can undermine the overall effectiveness of the educational environment.

Operant conditioning also plays a pivotal role in promoting self-regulated learning and motivation among students. By reinforcing effort, perseverance, and self-directed learning, educators can cultivate a sense of autonomy and intrinsic motivation within students. This can lead to increased engagement, improved academic performance, and a positive attitude towards learning.

Applications in Clinical Psychology

Clinicians utilize principles of operant conditioning to bring about positive behavioral changes in their clients. Through the application of reinforcement and punishment techniques, clinicians can address maladaptive behaviors and promote healthier psychological functioning. For example, in the treatment of anxiety disorders, systematic desensitization, a form of operant conditioning, is often employed to help individuals overcome their fears and anxieties. By gradually exposing patients to their feared stimuli while encouraging relaxation and coping strategies, clinicians apply the principles of operant conditioning to help patients reframe their responses to anxiety-provoking situations. Additionally, in the treatment of substance use disorders, operant conditioning techniques are widely used to reinforce abstinence and discourage substance-seeking behaviors. Behavioral therapies such as contingency management offer a structured approach to incentivize sobriety through positive reinforcement. Moreover, operant conditioning principles are integrated into therapeutic interventions for children with developmental disabilities. Clinicians work collaboratively with families and educators to implement behavior modification plans that incorporate positive reinforcement strategies to cultivate desired behaviors and mitigate challenging ones. This collaborative and customized approach exemplifies the versatility and efficacy of operant conditioning applications in clinical psychology. Furthermore, in the context of mood disorders, operant conditioning interventions are tailored to address specific depressive or manic symptoms. By structuring the environment to promote engagement in rewarding activities, clinicians leverage operant conditioning to increase adaptive behaviors and reduce aversive ones. Ultimately, the integration of operant conditioning principles within clinical psychology underscores its relevance in addressing a wide array of psychological disorders and enhancing overall well-being. The utilization of evidence-based behavior modification techniques rooted in operant conditioning not only reflects the dynamic nature of clinical psychology but also highlights the potential for fostering meaningful and lasting change in individuals' lives.

The Role of Operant Conditioning in Workplace Behavior

By understanding the principles of operant conditioning, employers and managers can effectively shape employee behaviors to align with the goals and values of the organization. One key aspect of operant conditioning in the workplace is the use of reinforcement to encourage desirable behaviors. Positive reinforcement involves rewarding employees for demonstrating desired behaviors, such as meeting performance targets, displaying teamwork, or demonstrating leadership skills. By providing positive reinforcement, organizations can motivate employees to consistently exhibit behaviors that contribute to productivity and overall success. Conversely, negative reinforcement involves removing aversive stimuli when the desired behavior is exhibited, further reinforcing the desired actions.

In addition to reinforcement, the strategic use of punishment also influences workplace behavior. Employers may implement punishment, such as reprimands or disciplinary actions, to decrease the occurrence of undesirable behaviors in the workplace. It is essential to note that the application of punishment should be carefully considered and applied judiciously to avoid creating a negative work environment. Understanding the appropriate timing and consistency of punishment is crucial in mitigating adverse effects on employee morale and motivation.

The concept of extinction is relevant in addressing unwanted behaviors in the workplace. When certain behaviors are no longer reinforced, they may gradually diminish or become extinct. For example, if an employee engages in disruptive behavior to seek attention, withholding reinforcement for such actions can lead to a reduction in the behavior over time.

Effective implementation of operant conditioning in the workplace requires a deep understanding of individual differences and the impact of environmental factors on behavior. Managers should consider the unique preferences and motivators of their employees when designing reinforcement strategies. Moreover, creating a supportive and nurturing work environment can enhance the effectiveness of operant conditioning techniques, fostering a culture of continuous improvement and mutual respect.

Parenting Techniques and Behavioral Outcomes

Operant conditioning principles can be effectively applied in the field of parenting to encourage desirable behaviors and discourage undesirable ones. When parents implement consistent reinforcement strategies, they are essentially shaping their child's behavior through operant conditioning. For instance, the use of positive reinforcement, such as verbal praise or rewards, when a child exhibits positive behaviors, can strengthen those behaviors over time. Conversely, the judicious use of punishment, in the form of consequences for negative behaviors, can aid in discouraging unwanted conduct. It is crucial for parents to understand that the effectiveness of these techniques lies in their consistency and appropriateness. Consistency reinforces the desired behaviors and clarity in communication regarding expectations and consequences. Furthermore, applying operant conditioning in parenting also involves understanding the concept of shaping, where gradual reinforcement guides the child towards more complex and desirable behaviors. This technique allows children to progress systematically in their behavioral development. Additionally, the use of extinction, where certain behaviors are not reinforced and eventually diminish, is another aspect that parents should consider when employing operant conditioning in parenting. It is important to note that successful implementation of these techniques requires a delicate balance between warmth, support, and structure within the parent-child relationship. Research has shown that positive parenting approaches based on operant conditioning principles can lead to improved self-regulation, social competence, and overall well-being in children

Animal Training and Behavioral Reinforcement

Animal training and behavioral reinforcement constitute prominent domains where the principles of operant conditioning are extensively employed. Animal trainers across various disciplines, from marine mammal trainers at aquatic parks to dog trainers working with K-9 units, rely on operant conditioning techniques to shape behaviors for specific tasks and performances.

One of the fundamental aspects of animal training is understanding the significance of positive reinforcement. By associating a desired behavior, such as performing a trick or responding to a command, with a positive consequence, such as receiving a food reward or verbal praise, trainers effectively reinforce the behavior, increasing the likelihood of its recurrence. This method aligns with B.F. Skinner's principles of reinforcement, emphasizing the importance of consequences in modifying behavior.

The concept of extinction, wherein undesired behaviors are gradually eliminated by withholding reinforcement, plays a pivotal role in animal training. Trainers meticulously identify instances when undesirable behaviors occur, strategically ceasing any form of reinforcement, thereby diminishing the likelihood of the behavior being displayed in the future.

In addition to positive reinforcement, operant conditioning also encompasses the application of negative reinforcement in animal training. Negative reinforcement involves removing an aversive stimulus upon displaying the desired behavior, thus strengthening the likelihood of the behavior reoccurring. Through careful implementation of negative reinforcement, trainers can effectively shape behavior while fostering a positive training environment.

The concept of shaping, a technique used to progressively achieve complex behaviors by reinforcing successive approximations, is a cornerstone of animal training. Trainers break down behaviors into manageable steps, reinforcing each incremental progress until the desired behavior is achieved. This process exemplifies the potency of operant conditioning in eliciting complex performances from animals.

The successful application of operant conditioning in animal training extends beyond domesticated pets to include exotic animals in zoological facilities and wildlife conservation centers. From training birds of prey to participate in public demonstrations to facilitating the rehabilitation of injured or orphaned wildlife, the principles of operant conditioning serve as a powerful tool in promoting the welfare and cooperation of various animal species.

Technological Integration in Behavioral Modification

Technological innovations have revolutionized the field of behavioral modification, offering unprecedented opportunities to enhance the effectiveness and precision of behavior change interventions. The integration of technology in behavioral modification strategies has not only expanded the scope of applications but has also significantly improved the monitoring, assessment, and delivery of interventions. One of the pivotal contributions of technology in behavioral modification is the development of sophisticated data collection and analysis tools. These tools enable practitioners to gather real-time and longitudinal data on behavioral patterns, facilitating a comprehensive understanding of the targeted behaviors and their responses to interventions. Furthermore, technological advancements have led to the creation of wearable devices and mobile applications that allow individuals to self-monitor their behaviors, receive feedback, and engage in interactive interventions, thereby promoting autonomy and self-regulation.

The utilization of virtual reality (VR) and augmented reality (AR) platforms has opened new avenues for simulating real-life scenarios and providing exposure therapy in controlled environments. This immersive technology has been particularly beneficial in addressing phobias, anxiety disorders, and post-traumatic stress disorder (PTSD) by creating customizable and safe environments for gradual desensitization and positive reinforcement. Additionally, the integration of gamification principles in behavioral modification apps has demonstrated promising results in sustaining user engagement and motivation, encouraging adherence to intervention protocols, and fostering behavior change through rewarding experiences.

Another significant area of technological integration in behavioral modification is the application of artificial intelligence (AI) and machine learning algorithms to personalize interventions and predictive modeling. By analyzing vast datasets and identifying patterns, AI-enabled systems can tailor interventions to individual needs, anticipate barriers to behavior change, and optimize reinforcement schedules. Furthermore, telehealth platforms have extended the reach of behavioral modification interventions, enabling remote delivery of services, continuous communication between practitioners and clients, and overcoming geographical barriers to accessing care. This has been especially crucial in ensuring equitable and inclusive provision of behavioral interventions across diverse populations and communities.

In conclusion, the integration of technology in behavioral modification represents a paradigm shift in the way interventions are designed, implemented, and evaluated. From empowering individuals through self-monitoring tools to leveraging artificial intelligence for personalized interventions, technological integration continues to propel the field of behavioral modification towards greater efficacy, accessibility, and innovation.

KEY EXPERIMENTS IN OPERANT CONDITIONING

The Operant Chamber

B.F. Skinner's operant chamber, also known as the Skinner box, is a fundamental apparatus in the field of operant conditioning, designed to study the relationship between behavior and its consequences. This controlled environment allowed Skinner to conduct groundbreaking experiments that provided invaluable insights into the principles of operant conditioning. Among the key findings from Skinner's work include the demonstration of how the use of reinforcement schedules, such as fixed ratio or variable interval schedules, can shape and maintain specific behaviors. Moreover, Skinner's research highlighted the significance of positive and negative reinforcement in modulating behavior through the systematic manipulation of environmental contingencies. The operant chamber's innovative design enabled researchers to precisely measure and record an organism's behavioral responses, paving the way for quantitative analysis and rigorous experimentation. Additionally, Skinner's investigations elucidated the concept of shaping behavior through successive approximations, a technique that remains integral in behavior modification interventions. By systematically altering the reinforcement schedule within the operant chamber, Skinner was able to illustrate the complex dynamics of behavior acquisition and maintenance, offering empirical support for operant conditioning principles. Furthermore, Skinner's seminal work with the operant chamber led to advancements in behavioral technology, facilitating the automation of reinforcement delivery and data collection, which revolutionized the experimental study of behavior. His meticulous documentation and analysis of operant behavior within the chamber not only expanded our understanding of behavioral principles but also set the stage for subsequent research exploring the neural mechanisms underlying operant conditioning.

Variable Ratio and Interval Schedules in Practice

In the field of operant conditioning, variable ratio and interval schedules play an important role in shaping and maintaining behavioral responses. These schedules introduce an element of unpredictability, which has been found to strongly influence the frequency and stability of behaviors. In practice, understanding and effectively utilizing these schedules can have wide-ranging implications in various fields such as education, business, and psychology.

Variable ratio schedules involve reinforcing a behavior after an unpredictable number of responses. This schedule is highly effective in promoting high rates of responding and reducing the likelihood of extinction. For instance, in educational settings, employing variable ratio schedules can enhance student engagement and motivation by intermittently rewarding their participation or academic efforts. Similarly, in the field of business and marketing, implementing variable ratio schedules in reward programs or loyalty initiatives can foster continued consumer patronage and active participation.

On the other hand, variable interval schedules reinforce a behavior after varying time intervals, again introducing an element of unpredictability. This schedule has been observed to produce steady and consistent rates of responding with minimal instances of post-reinforcement pauses. Applying variable interval schedules in therapeutic interventions or behavior modification programs allows for the maintenance of desired behaviors over extended periods. Moreover, in organizational management, utilizing variable interval schedules can promote sustained employee performance by providing intermittent and unpredictable reinforcement for exemplary work.

It is noteworthy that both variable ratio and interval schedules are inherently different from fixed schedules, wherein the predictability of reinforcement leads to distinct patterns of behavior. The practical implications of these variable schedules extend beyond individual behavior modification to broader societal contexts, contributing to the development of effective interventions and programs in diverse professional domains.

Research into the implementation and optimization of variable schedules continues to advance, shedding light on the nuanced mechanisms underlying behavioral reinforcement and maintenance. This evolving understanding holds promise for refining existing practices and innovating strategies aimed at fostering enduring behavioral change across diverse settings.

The Cumulative Recorder

The cumulative recorder, a device developed by B.F. Skinner for his operant conditioning experiments, has revolutionized the study of behavioral changes. This sophisticated instrument allows researchers to precisely and continuously record an organism's behavior over time, providing valuable insights into patterns and trends. The cumulative recorder operates by graphing the cumulative number of responses made by the subject versus time on a continuous paper tape, creating a visual representation of the rate and variability of behavior.

One of the key advantages of the cumulative recorder is its ability to objectively capture and display data in real-time, eliminating the need for manual observation and human error. By analyzing the resulting graphs, researchers can identify distinct behavioral patterns, such as steady rates of responding, sudden shifts, or periods of high and low activity. This granular level of detail enables a deeper understanding of how environmental cues and reinforcement schedules influence behavior.

The cumulative recorder has been instrumental in validating operant conditioning principles and demonstrating the effectiveness of reinforcement and punishment techniques. Through carefully designed experiments, researchers have used this tool to explore the impact of different reinforcement schedules, such as fixed ratio or variable interval, on subjects' response rates and endurance. These studies have provided empirical evidence supporting the robustness and applicability of operant conditioning across various contexts and species.

In addition to laboratory settings, the cumulative recorder has also found practical applications in fields such as education, psychology, and animal training. Teachers and educators have utilized this technology to assess student engagement and learning progress, using the recorded data to tailor instructional strategies and interventions. Similarly, behavior analysts have leveraged the cumulative recorder to document and analyze behavioral changes in clinical and therapeutic settings, informing personalized treatment plans for individuals with developmental disorders or maladaptive behaviors.

As research methods continue to advance, the cumulative recorder remains an indispensable tool for investigating the dynamics of behavior. Its precision and versatility make it a cornerstone of behavioral research, facilitating the exploration of complex phenomena and the development of evidence-based interventions. Looking forward, ongoing advancements in technology will likely enhance the capabilities of the cumulative recorder, opening new frontiers for understanding and influencing behavior.

Punishment's Exploration through Laboratory Experiments

In laboratory experiments, researchers utilize controlled settings to observe the effects of punishment on behavioral responses. These experiments aim to elucidate the mechanisms behind punishment, providing valuable insights into its effectiveness and ethical implications. Through carefully designed studies, scientists have been able to identify the varied ways in which punishment influences behavior.

One significant focus of these laboratory experiments is the analysis of different types of punishment, including positive punishment and negative punishment. By subjecting subjects to specific aversive stimuli or the removal of desirable stimuli contingent upon certain behaviors, researchers can systematically evaluate the impact of punishment on behavior. Such experiments allow for the quantification and analysis of behavioral changes in response to punitive measures.

Laboratory experiments delve into the factors that modulate the effectiveness of punishment. These investigations seek to determine the optimal timing, intensity, and consistency of punitive measures to yield desired behavioral outcomes. Through careful manipulation of these variables, researchers can discern patterns and principles governing the nuanced interplay between punishment and behavior.

Ethical considerations are paramount in the design and implementation of laboratory experiments pertaining to punishment. Researchers must ensure that subjects are treated with respect and that potential harm is minimized. Ethical guidelines govern the use of punishment in experimental settings, emphasizing the importance of informed consent and the well-being of participants. Additionally, the responsible and judicious application of punishment aligns with ethical standards and furthers our understanding of its implications.

The outcomes of laboratory experiments on punishment have far-reaching applications beyond the confines of research environments. Insights garnered from these studies extend to educational institutions, clinical settings, and diverse real-world contexts. The findings serve as a foundation for formulating evidence-based strategies for behavioral intervention, facilitating the effective management of challenging behaviors.

Translational Research

Translational research in the field of operant conditioning constitutes a pivotal link between controlled laboratory environments and the practical applications of behavioral principles in real-world settings. This essential bridge aims to translate the findings and insights gained from rigorous experimental studies into tangible strategies for addressing behavior in everyday contexts. Through an interdisciplinary approach that integrates psychology, education, and various other fields, translational research seeks to enhance the relevance and impact of operant conditioning in diverse domains.

One key aspect of translational research involves identifying the transferability of experimental results to naturalistic settings. Researchers meticulously explore how the principles of operant conditioning established in laboratory environments can be adapted and implemented effectively in educational, clinical, and organizational settings. By studying the applicability of reinforcement schedules, shaping techniques, and behavioral interventions across different contexts, translational research sheds light on the nuances and complexities of behavior change in the real world.

Translational research endeavors to address the practical challenges associated with applying experimental findings in diverse social and cultural settings. This involves considering factors such as individual differences, societal norms, and ethical considerations that may influence the implementation of operant conditioning paradigms outside the laboratory. By examining these contextual variables, researchers aim to develop culturally sensitive and ethically sound approaches to behavior modification that resonate with diverse populations.

Another critical function of translational research is to facilitate the dissemination of evidence-based practices derived from operant conditioning principles. Through collaborations with practitioners, educators, and policymakers, translational researchers play a vital role in translating complex behavioral concepts into accessible interventions and programs. By disseminating knowledge through workshops, training sessions, and educational materials, they empower professionals to integrate evidence-based behavioral strategies into their work, thus maximizing the impact of operant conditioning principles.

Ethical Considerations in Experimental Design

The ethical framework governing experimental design encompasses various dimensions, including but not limited to ensuring the welfare and well-being of research subjects, promoting transparency and informed consent, and upholding integrity in data collection and analysis. Additionally, it involves safeguarding against potential harm, physical or psychological, that may arise from participating in experimental protocols. The ethical guidelines set forth by professional bodies and institutional review boards serve as the cornerstone for researchers to navigate these complex considerations. Ensuring respect for autonomy, beneficence, non-maleficence, and justice forms the fundamental essence of ethical experimental design in operant conditioning research.

When considering the operationalization of ethical standards in experimental design, researchers must actively integrate principles of fairness, equity, and respect for individual autonomy. Crucially, obtaining voluntary and fully informed consent from research participants stands as a non-negotiable imperative. This involves clearly and comprehensively disclosing the aims, procedures, potential risks, and benefits associated with the study. Moreover, researchers need to be vigilant in minimizing any coercion or undue influence on participants in the recruitment and conduct of experiments. Striking a balance between scientific rigor and ethical responsibility necessitates ongoing examination of potential risks and benefits, as well as proactive measures to mitigate any adverse consequences.

Ethical experimental design in operant conditioning research entails a keen focus on ensuring the humane treatment of laboratory animals, where applicable. Adherence to established guidelines for animal care and use is paramount in upholding ethical standards within this domain. This involves meticulous attention to housing conditions, veterinary care, and minimizing distress or discomfort experienced by the animals during experimental procedures. Furthermore, researchers are entrusted with the responsibility of continually assessing the necessity and justification for employing animal models, while consistently striving to explore alternative methodologies to minimize animal use and suffering whenever feasible.

Beyond the core tenets of ethical experimental design lie the imperatives of data integrity and responsible dissemination of findings. The ethical conduct of research extends to the transparent and accurate reporting of methods, results, and interpretations, thereby enabling critical appraisal and replication by the broader scientific community. Upholding the principles of scientific integrity, honesty, and objectivity serves to fortify public trust and confidence in the field of operant conditioning research. Consequently, researchers bear the ethical obligation to demonstrate unwavering commitment to truthfulness and ethical practice throughout all facets of the experimental endeavor.

By conscientiously integrating ethical considerations into the fabric of experimental design, operant conditioning researchers can uphold the highest moral and professional standards while advancing the frontiers of knowledge. Embracing an ethical compass not only safeguards the rights and well-being of research participants and subjects but also enhances the credibility and impact of the research outcomes. Ethical experimental design stands as an indispensable pillar underpinning the advancement of operant conditioning research, serving to elevate its societal relevance and ethical probity.

Longitudinal Studies

Longitudinal studies involve observing and analyzing the same individuals repeatedly over extended periods, allowing researchers to track the developmental trajectories of behavior, identify patterns of change and stability, and explore causal factors that influence these patterns. The comprehensive nature of longitudinal studies allows for the examination of behavioral variations within an individual, shedding light on the dynamic interplay between environmental influences and inherent traits. By documenting behavioral changes across various life stages, researchers can discern critical periods and milestones associated with behavioral development, offering profound implications for intervention and support programs. Furthermore, longitudinal studies enable the detection of long-term effects of interventions or environmental exposures, contributing to our understanding of the lasting impact of early experiences on behavior. This research approach also provides valuable data for evaluating the effectiveness of behavioral interventions and identifying potential predictors of positive outcomes. However, conducting longitudinal studies poses numerous methodological challenges, such as participant attrition, data collection consistency, and managing the influence of external variables. Ethical considerations regarding participant welfare, consent, and privacy are also paramount in longitudinal research, emphasizing the need for rigorous ethical protocols and ongoing ethical review. Despite these challenges, longitudinal studies remain pivotal in advancing our comprehension of behavioral dynamics and facilitating evidence-based decision-making in diverse domains, including education, clinical psychology, and public policy. As technology and statistical methodologies continue to evolve, the potential for longitudinal studies to elucidate the complexities of human behavior and inform interventions is ever-expanding. Future advancements in data collection techniques, such as wearable sensors and ecological momentary assessment, hold promise for enhancing the precision and granularity of longitudinal behavioral data, opening new avenues for investigating behavior in naturalistic settings. Similarly, advances in statistical modeling and data analysis offer opportunities to extract richer insights from longitudinal datasets by unraveling temporal patterns in behavior and identifying latent constructs underlying behavioral changes.

Innovations and Future Directions in Operant Conditioning Research

As we progress further into the current century, the field of operant conditioning research is witnessing an array of innovative advancements and exciting future directions that promise to expand our understanding of behavior modification and its applications. One key area of innovation lies in the integration of technology, particularly the use of advanced data analytics and machine learning algorithms to analyze behavioral patterns and predict responses more accurately. This approach not only offers novel insights into behavior but also enhances the precision and efficacy of interventions. Furthermore, the emergence of virtual reality (VR) as a tool for simulating real-life environments opens up new possibilities for studying behavior in controlled yet immersive settings. Researchers are now harnessing VR to create scenarios that allow for precise manipulation of environmental stimuli, offering unparalleled opportunities for studying behavioral responses.

Another promising direction in operant conditioning research pertains to interdisciplinary collaborations. By forging partnerships with fields such as neuroscience, genetics, and cognitive psychology, researchers are gaining fresh perspectives on the underlying mechanisms of behavioral change. This interdisciplinary approach has the potential to uncover previously unexplored factors influencing behavior and develop comprehensive models of behavior modification. Moreover, the growing emphasis on personalized medicine in healthcare has spurred interest in tailoring behavioral interventions to individual characteristics, such as genetic predispositions and neurobiological profiles. Integrating genomic and neuroimaging data into operant conditioning research holds immense promise for optimizing treatment outcomes and designing targeted interventions.

In addition to these technological and interdisciplinary strides, the ethical dimensions of operant conditioning research continue to evolve. With heightened awareness of ethical considerations in behavioral experimentation, there is a concerted effort to ensure that research practices prioritize the welfare and autonomy of participants. This ethical imperative drives the exploration of alternative research methodologies that minimize discomfort and stress in experimental subjects while yielding robust data. Moreover, discussions around the responsible use of behavioral interventions and the implications of long-term behavioral modification are shaping the ethical landscape of operant conditioning research, prompting critical reflections among practitioners and scholars.

Looking ahead, the future of operant conditioning research is poised to witness a convergence of scientific innovation, multidisciplinary collaboration, and ethical conscientiousness, leading to transformative breakthroughs with far-reaching implications for behavioral science and practical applications across diverse domains.

SCHEDULES OF REINFORCEMENT

Continuous vs. Partial Reinforcement

Reinforcement schedules are fundamental to the understanding of operant conditioning and its applications in behavioral psychology. These schedules govern the timing and frequency of reinforcement delivery, thereby influencing the strength and persistence of learned behaviors. Understanding reinforcement schedules is crucial as they play a pivotal role in shaping behavior and determining the effectiveness of behavioral interventions. Continuous reinforcement involves providing a reward every time a desired behavior occurs. This approach is effective in establishing new behaviors as the individual consistently receives reinforcement for their actions. However, it can also lead to quicker extinction if the reinforcement is suddenly discontinued. On the other hand, partial reinforcement, also known as intermittent reinforcement, entails providing reinforcement only some of the time when the desired behavior is displayed. This method often results in more persistent behavior as the individual learns that the reward may not always be immediate, leading to continued efforts to obtain the reinforcement. Moreover, partial reinforcement schedules can be based on multiple criteria, including fixed ratio, variable ratio, fixed interval, or variable interval, each impacting the frequency and pattern of reinforcement delivery. Studies have shown that behaviors reinforced under partial reinforcement schedules are more resistant to extinction, making them particularly relevant in real-world scenarios where consistent reinforcement may not always be feasible. Importantly, understanding the distinction between continuous and partial reinforcement provides valuable insights into the mechanisms that govern behavioral maintenance and longevity.

Fixed-Ratio Schedule - Consistency and Impact

Fixed-ratio schedules are characterized by the consistent delivery of reinforcement following a predetermined number of responses. This schedule fosters a pattern of behavior where the subject tends to increase their response rate as they anticipate reaching the specified ratio, leading to more frequent occurrences of the desired behavior.

One of the defining features of fixed-ratio schedules is their predictability. The consistent nature of reinforcement following a specific number of responses creates a clear link between the behavior and its consequences, shaping the subject's understanding of the relationship between their actions and the expected outcome. This predictability often results in high response rates, as individuals strive to meet the required criteria for reinforcement, thereby demonstrating the influence of fixed-ratio schedules on behavioral patterns.

The impact of fixed-ratio schedules extends beyond the immediate reinforcement phase. Through consistent reinforcement at set intervals, individuals are likely to exhibit persistent and rapid responses, reflecting the enduring effects of this schedule on behavior. The reinforcement schedule also facilitates the acquisition and maintenance of complex behaviors, as it encourages individuals to engage in repetitive actions to achieve the established ratio, thus promoting skill development and proficiency in specific tasks.

In practical applications, fixed-ratio schedules are employed across diverse fields such as education, business, and clinical settings. In educational contexts, teachers utilize fixed-ratio schedules to reinforce students' learning efforts, ensuring that mastery of certain skills or completion of designated tasks is consistently rewarded after a specific number of correct responses. Similarly, in the business field, sales incentives and commission-based structures often adhere to fixed-ratio schedules, motivating employees to demonstrate heightened performance and productivity to attain the set reinforcement criteria.

Variable-Ratio Schedule - Randomization in Practice

The Variable-Ratio (VR) schedule is quintessential in the field of operant conditioning, characterized by the delivery of reinforcement after a variable number of responses. Unlike fixed ratio or interval schedules, in VR schedules, the exact number of responses required to receive reinforcement varies, lending an element of unpredictability to the reinforcement process. This unpredictability often leads to high and consistent rates of responding, making VR schedules particularly effective in maintaining desired behaviors. Psychologically, the variability in the reinforcement timing keeps the individual engaged and motivated to continue performing the target behavior, as they are uncertain about when the reinforcement will occur. This leads to persistence in the behavior and resilience to extinction. The VR schedule closely resembles many real-world situations where rewards are not delivered on a fixed schedule, such as gambling or sales commissions. In these scenarios, the intermittent reinforcement created by VR schedules can lead to habitual and persistent behaviors. It is essential for practitioners and researchers to understand the implications of VR schedules in various contexts, including addiction and consumer behavior. Studies have shown that VR schedules are significantly associated with addictive behaviors, as individuals become conditioned to expect rewards after a variable number of attempts, leading to compulsive engagement despite limited reinforcement. Furthermore, in marketing and sales, incorporating elements of variability in reward delivery can influence consumer purchasing behavior and brand loyalty. Understanding the impact of VR schedules is crucial for maintaining ethical practices and avoiding manipulative strategies in consumer engagement. While VR schedules have proven efficacy in maintaining behaviors, it is imperative to carefully consider their applications, particularly in fields where ethical considerations are paramount.

Fixed-Interval Schedule - Timed Reinforcement Patterns

Fixed-interval schedule refers to a pattern of reinforcement where a response is only reinforced after a specific amount of time has elapsed. This type of schedule creates an interesting dynamic in behavior as the reinforcement is not contingent on the frequency of responses but rather on the passage of time. It leads to predictable patterns of responding, with an increase in responding as the reinforcement time approaches. However, there is often a decrease in responding immediately after the reinforcement is delivered, followed by a gradual increase as the next reinforcement time draws nearer.

Research has shown that organisms tend to exhibit a scalloped response pattern under fixed-interval schedules, where there is minimal responding right after reinforcement and a rapid increase in responding as the reinforcement time approaches. This phenomenon can be observed in various contexts, from animal studies to human behavior, and has implications in understanding how time-based reinforcements impact learning and behavior.

In applications, fixed-interval schedules have been utilized in diverse settings, ranging from animal training to workplace incentives. Understanding the dynamics of fixed-interval schedules allows for effective utilization of timed reinforcement patterns. For example, in employee performance management, rewarding workers on a fixed-interval schedule may lead to increased productivity as individuals strive to meet the timing criteria for reinforcement.

The consistent pace of behavior under fixed-interval schedules can be advantageous in establishing routines and predictability. In educational settings, teachers may employ fixed-interval schedules to reinforce student engagement over set time intervals, promoting sustained attention and participation in learning activities. Additionally, the use of fixed-interval schedules in therapeutic interventions, such as addiction treatment programs, underscores the value of timed reinforcements in shaping and maintaining desired behaviors.

Variable-Interval Schedule - Unpredictable Timing

In contrast to fixed-interval schedules, variable-interval schedules involve reinforcement provided at unpredictable time intervals. This unpredictability poses a unique challenge for the subject, as they are unable to anticipate when the next reinforcement will occur. This results in a steady rate of responding, as the individual is consistently engaged in the desired behavior, not knowing when their effort will be rewarded. The variability in timing prevents the development of specific patterns or expectations, leading to a more sustained and stable response pattern. The unpredictable nature of variable-interval schedules closely mirrors many real-life scenarios, making it an important concept with wide-ranging applications. From educational settings to behavioral therapy, understanding and implementing variable-interval schedules can have significant impacts. In educational contexts, teachers can use this schedule to encourage continuous engagement and active participation among students. By incorporating unpredictable timing of positive reinforcements, educators can foster consistent attention and motivation in the learning environment. Furthermore, in behavioral therapy, variable-interval schedules can be utilized to promote ongoing engagement in therapeutic activities and behaviors. This can contribute to the overall effectiveness of interventions, ensuring that individuals remain consistently engaged in their treatment plan. Moreover, in organizational settings, variable-interval schedules can be employed to maintain employee productivity and motivation. By creating an environment where rewards are provided at unpredictable intervals, employers can cultivate sustained effort and commitment among their workforce. The impact of variable-interval schedules extends beyond basic operant conditioning principles, permeating various facets of human behavior and interaction. Additionally, the incorporation of randomization in reinforcement schedules has implications for exploring the dynamics of motivation and persistence.

Reinforcement Schedules' Comparison

In the field of operant conditioning, a critical aspect lies in the comparative analysis of different reinforcement schedules. Understanding and dissecting these schedules enables a deeper comprehension of how behavior is shaped and maintained. A prominent comparison exists between fixed-ratio (FR) and variable-ratio (VR) schedules, with the former entailing a consistent number of responses before reinforcement, while the latter involves reinforcement after an unpredictable number of responses. This dichotomy prompts an evaluation of their respective impact on behavior. Fixed-interval (FI) and variable-interval (VI) schedules similarly warrant examination, as the former denotes reinforcement at set time intervals and the latter involves reinforcement after varying time periods. Comparing these schedules underscores the significance of timing variability in reinforcing behavior. The effectiveness of each schedule in promoting certain behaviors or yielding resistance to extinction further underscores the importance of comparative analysis. Moreover, considering the predictability or unpredictability of reinforcement across schedules elicits fundamental differences in behavioral responses. By scrutinizing factors such as response rates, resistance to extinction, and patterns of behavior acquisition, a nuanced understanding of each reinforcement schedule emerges. Additionally, exploring the utility of these schedules in distinct settings – such as educational environments, clinical interventions, and animal training – unveils their practical implications. Behavioral therapies often leverage this comparative analysis to tailor interventions and achieve desired outcomes for patients. Furthermore, examining the interaction between reinforcement schedules and individual differences in responding offers key insights into behavior modification strategies customized for diverse populations.

Real-world Applications

Real-world applications of reinforcement schedules are pervasive and have demonstrated significant impact in various fields.

In the field of education, researchers and educators have utilized reinforcement schedules to enhance students' learning experiences. By implementing variable-ratio schedules in classroom settings, teachers can effectively promote sustained engagement and participation among students, ultimately improving academic performance. Furthermore, in organizational behavior management, the judicious use of reinforcement schedules has been instrumental in shaping desirable employee behaviors and fostering a positive work culture. Through the strategic application of reinforcement schedules, businesses have succeeded in increasing productivity, reducing absenteeism, and cultivating a motivated workforce. Additionally, within clinical psychology and behavioral therapy, reinforcement schedules have proven indispensable in addressing maladaptive behaviors and promoting adaptive responses. Case studies have highlighted the efficacy of using intermittent reinforcement schedules to mitigate addictive behaviors, such as substance abuse, and to facilitate long-term behavior change. Moreover, in animal training and wildlife conservation, reinforcement schedules play a crucial role in shaping behaviors for diverse species. From training domestic pets to modifying behaviors of endangered animals in conservation efforts, reinforcement schedules offer a consistent and ethical approach to behavior modification. These real-world applications underscore the versatility and effectiveness of reinforcement schedules across a spectrum of disciplines, positioning them as valuable tools for behavior management and modification.

Implications for Behavioral Modification

Understanding the implications of reinforcement schedules on behavior modification is crucial for professionals in fields such as clinical psychology, education, and organizational management. Reinforcement schedules provide insights into how behaviors can be maintained, shaped, and ultimately modified to achieve desired outcomes. By comprehending the varying effects of different reinforcement schedules, practitioners can adeptly design interventions tailored to specific behavioral patterns.

The application of reinforcement schedules in behavioral modification transcends individual contexts and extends to diverse settings. In clinical psychology, for instance, understanding the impact of variable-ratio schedules on substance abuse cessation programs facilitates the development of more effective treatment plans. Similarly, in educational settings, the strategic implementation of fixed-interval schedules can enhance student motivation and engagement through consistent reinforcement of desired academic behaviors.

The implications of reinforcement schedules in behavioral modification are evident in organizational management practices. Businesses utilize these principles to promote workplace productivity, incentivize performance improvements, and facilitate skill development among employees. By recognizing the effectiveness of reinforcement schedules, leaders can create a work environment conducive to sustained behavioral change and continuous professional growth.

Behavioral modification strategies informed by reinforcement schedules play a pivotal role in addressing challenging behaviors across varied populations. Whether working with individuals with developmental disorders, implementing behavior management plans in schools, or devising interventions for individuals struggling with compulsive behaviors, the nuanced understanding of reinforcement schedules empowers practitioners to tailor interventions that yield enduring results.

EXPERIMENTAL ANALYSIS OF BEHAVIOR

Behavioral Research Methodologies

Behavioral research methodologies encompass a range of approaches and techniques aimed at systematically observing, measuring, and understanding behavior in controlled environments. These methodologies are fundamental to the experimental analysis of behavior, providing researchers with the tools to investigate the variables that influence human and animal actions. One of the primary methodologies employed in behavioral research is the use of controlled experiments. These experiments typically involve the manipulation of specific environmental or situational factors to observe their impact on behavior. By meticulously controlling the conditions in which behavior occurs, researchers can isolate and measure the effects of various stimuli, responses, and consequences. Another widely utilized methodology is systematic observation, which involves the careful and structured recording of behaviors in natural or controlled settings. This approach allows researchers to document behavioral patterns, identify correlations, and formulate hypotheses for further investigation. Behavioral surveys and interviews are also instrumental in gathering qualitative data related to attitudes, beliefs, and experiences that may influence behavior. Additionally, technological advancements have introduced innovative methodologies such as neuroimaging and biometric measurements, enabling researchers to explore the neural and physiological underpinnings of behavior. Understanding the ethical considerations that govern behavioral research is crucial. Researchers must adhere to strict ethical guidelines to ensure the well-being and rights of participants, as well as the responsible conduct of their studies. Informed consent, confidentiality, and the minimization of potential harm are essential principles that guide the design and implementation of behavioral research. Moreover, peer review and oversight by institutional review boards serve to uphold the integrity and ethical standards of behavioral studies.

Key Experiments and Discoveries

Operant conditioning has been the subject of numerous key experiments and groundbreaking discoveries that have significantly contributed to our understanding of behavior and learning. As previously stated, one of the pivotal experiments was conducted by B.F. Skinner himself, who developed the concept of the Skinner Box, also known as an operant chamber. Through this experiment, Skinner demonstrated the powerful influence of positive and negative reinforcement on shaping and maintaining behaviors.

Another significant discovery in the field of operant conditioning was made by psychologist Edward Thorndike, who formulated the Law of Effect. This principle asserted that behaviors followed by favorable consequences are more likely to be repeated, while those followed by unfavorable consequences are less likely to occur in the future. Thorndike's work laid the theoretical groundwork for the development of operant conditioning and provided valuable insights into the relationship between behavior and its consequences.

The research conducted by Burrhus Frederic (B.F.) Skinner led to the identification of various schedules of reinforcement, which significantly influenced subsequent studies in operant conditioning. Skinner's pioneering work involved exploring different patterns of reinforcement delivery and their impact on behavior. The findings from these experiments revealed the differential effects of continuous reinforcement, fixed ratio schedules, variable ratio schedules, fixed interval schedules, and variable interval schedules on behavioral responses.

The work of behavioral psychologists such as John B. Watson and Ivan Pavlov also contributed to the foundational knowledge of operant conditioning. While Watson focused on the principles of classical conditioning, his research laid the groundwork for the future development of operant conditioning theories. Similarly, Pavlov's experiments with canine salivation responses elucidated the importance of associative learning, providing valuable insights into the mechanisms of behavior modification and control.

Contemporary research in the field of operant conditioning continues to produce new findings and refine existing theories. Recent studies have delved into areas such as stimulus control, discrimination training, and response shaping, shedding light on the processes underlying behavioral modification.

Data Collection and Analysis Techniques

The field of behavioral research necessitates the implementation of meticulous data collection and analysis techniques to derive meaningful insights from experimental studies. One fundamental aspect of data collection in operant conditioning experiments is the precise measurement of behaviors under investigation. Researchers employ various methods such as event recording, interval recording, and time sampling to accurately capture the frequency, duration, and intensity of specific behaviors exhibited by the subjects. Each of these methods offers distinct advantages and is chosen based on the nature of the behavior being studied.

Modern technology has revolutionized data collection in behavioral research. Advanced tools like video tracking systems, motion sensors, and specialized software enable researchers to automate the process of data acquisition, reducing human error and enhancing the precision of measurements. These technological advancements not only streamline the data collection process but also facilitate the monitoring of behaviors in diverse environmental settings, providing a comprehensive understanding of behavioral patterns.

In tandem with data collection, the analysis of collected data is crucial for drawing valid conclusions. Statistical techniques including descriptive statistics, inferential statistics, and graphical representation are commonly employed to analyze behavioral data. Descriptive statistics aid in summarizing and presenting the collected data, while inferential statistics enable researchers to make inferences and generalizations about the observed behaviors within the larger population. Additionally, graphical representation through histograms, line graphs, and scatter plots enhances the visual comprehension of behavioral trends and patterns.

The choice of appropriate statistical tests is paramount in determining the significance of experimental findings. Techniques such as t-tests, ANOVA, correlation analysis, and regression analysis provide valuable insights into the relationships between variables and the overall effectiveness of interventions. It is imperative for researchers to adhere to the principles of sound statistical analysis to ensure the validity and reliability of the study outcomes.

Ethical considerations also permeate the process of data collection and analysis in behavioral research. Protecting the welfare of the subjects, ensuring confidentiality, and obtaining informed consent are essential ethical considerations that guide the entire research endeavor. Striking an ethical balance while collecting and analyzing data is paramount to upholding the integrity and credibility of behavioral research.

Advancements in Experimental Apparatus

The evolution of technology has led to the development of sophisticated tools and equipment that have revolutionized the way behavioral experiments are conducted. One of the significant advancements in experimental apparatus is the integration of digital interfaces and automated data collection systems. This has streamlined the process of recording and analyzing behavioral data, allowing researchers to efficiently capture and interpret complex behavioral patterns. The utilization of advanced software and hardware components has enabled real-time monitoring and precise measurement of behavioral responses, leading to more accurate and reliable research outcomes.

The incorporation of virtual reality and augmented reality technologies has opened up new avenues for studying behavior in controlled environments. These immersive systems provide researchers with the ability to simulate various stimuli and environmental conditions, offering a higher degree of experimental control and manipulation. By creating realistic virtual scenarios, researchers can investigate behavioral responses in detail, providing valuable insights into the mechanisms underlying operant conditioning.

Advancements in neuroimaging techniques have also greatly contributed to the study of behavior through advanced experimental apparatus. Functional magnetic resonance imaging (fMRI) and electroencephalography (EEG) have enabled researchers to examine the neural correlates of behavior, shedding light on the neurological processes associated with operant conditioning. By integrating these neuroimaging technologies with behavioral experiments, researchers can elucidate the underlying neural mechanisms that govern behavioral responses, leading to a comprehensive understanding of operant behavior at the neurobiological level.

The development of state-of-the-art operant chambers and experimental setups has facilitated the precise control and manipulation of environmental stimuli and reinforcement schedules. These specialized apparatus allow for the systematic investigation of behavioral principles, such as reinforcement contingencies and stimulus discrimination, while ensuring rigorous experimental control. The integration of innovative features, such as customizable stimulus presentation and response tracking capabilities, has empowered researchers to design tailored experiments that address specific research questions and hypotheses.

Challenges and Limitations in Behavioral Research

Behavioral research, particularly within the context of operant conditioning, is a valuable field with significant potential for understanding human and animal behavior. However, it is important to recognize and address the challenges and limitations that researchers encounter in their pursuit of knowledge. One key challenge in behavioral research is the ethical considerations surrounding the use of animals in experiments. While animal studies have contributed crucial insights into learning and behavior, there is an ongoing ethical debate regarding the treatment of these subjects and the impact of experimental procedures on their welfare. Researchers must navigate this ethical landscape with care and diligence, ensuring that their work adheres to established guidelines and promotes the well-being of the animals involved. Another challenge lies in the complexity of behavior itself. Human and animal behavior is multifaceted and influenced by numerous variables, making it difficult to isolate specific causal relationships in experiments. This inherent complexity can present challenges in designing studies and interpreting results accurately. Additionally, the generalizability of findings from controlled laboratory settings to real-world environments poses a significant limitation. While controlled experiments provide valuable insights, applying these findings to complex, dynamic human and animal behaviors outside the laboratory setting requires careful consideration and often presents challenges. Methodological limitations also contribute to the challenges in behavioral research. Issues such as measurement precision, reliability of instruments, and standardization of experimental protocols can affect the validity and reproducibility of findings. Addressing these methodological challenges is essential for advancing the rigor and credibility of behavioral research. Furthermore, the interdisciplinary nature of behavioral research introduces challenges related to integrating findings from psychology, neuroscience, and other relevant fields. Collaborative efforts are necessary to bridge these disciplines and harness their collective expertise effectively. Finally, funding constraints and resource limitations can hinder the scope and scale of behavioral research initiatives, impacting the ability of researchers to explore complex behavioral phenomena comprehensively.

Behavioral Objectives and Outcomes in Education

By delineating specific, measurable, achievable, relevant, and time-bound (SMART) goals, educators can optimize the effectiveness of their instructional practices and interventions. Moreover, identifying and articulating these objectives enables teachers to align their teaching methods with the desired learning outcomes, fostering a more targeted and efficient educational process. Whether it involves improving academic performance, enhancing social behaviors, or refining cognitive skills, establishing clear behavioral objectives provides a roadmap for educators to tailor their approaches to suit individual student needs.

Through the application of operant conditioning principles, educators can address behavioral objectives in a systematic manner. By utilizing reinforcement strategies, such as positive reinforcement for desirable behaviors and negative reinforcement for the cessation of undesirable behaviors, teachers can shape and modify student conduct within the classroom environment. Additionally, the implementation of behavior modification techniques, including token economy systems and contingency management, empowers educators to foster positive behavioral changes and reinforce appropriate conduct among students.

The impact of defining behavioral objectives is reflected not only in individual student progress but also in the overall classroom dynamics and learning environment. When behavioral expectations are clearly communicated and consistently reinforced, students are more likely to exhibit the desired behaviors and engage actively in the learning process. Furthermore, by setting measurable benchmarks for behavioral outcomes, educators can monitor and assess the effectiveness of their interventions, enabling them to make informed adjustments to their instructional strategies and support mechanisms.

Addressing diverse behavioral objectives also necessitates a collaborative approach involving educators, parents, and support staff. By fostering open communication channels and aligning efforts, a more cohesive and comprehensive support system can be established, catering to the multifaceted needs of students. This inclusive approach not only promotes consistency in reinforcing behavioral objectives across different environments but also facilitates the seamless integration of behavioral strategies into various facets of a student's life, thereby maximizing the potential for holistic development.

Operant Techniques in Classroom Management

Operant conditioning provides valuable principles and techniques that can be applied to promote positive behavior and academic engagement among students. The use of reinforcement and punishment strategies can play a significant role in shaping student conduct within the classroom setting.

One key aspect of operant techniques in classroom management is the use of positive reinforcement. By providing rewards or incentives for desirable behaviors, educators can reinforce positive conduct and motivation in students. This can include praise, stickers, extra free time, or other forms of acknowledgment that are meaningful to the students. Implementing a system of rewards for good behavior not only encourages students to remain on task but also fosters a positive and supportive classroom atmosphere.

Negative reinforcement can also be utilized as a strategy for classroom management. Negative reinforcement involves the removal of an aversive stimulus following desired behavior, thereby increasing the likelihood of the behavior occurring again. For instance, if students are given extra recess time after completing their assignments promptly, they are more likely to continue completing tasks without delay. It's important to note that negative reinforcement differs from punishment, as it focuses on removing unpleasant stimuli rather than introducing them.

Alongside reinforcement, the concept of punishment should be approached with caution in the classroom environment. While punishment can modify behavior, its long-term effectiveness in promoting genuine understanding and intrinsic motivation is limited. Instead, alternative strategies such as time-out, loss of privileges, or logical consequences could be considered when addressing disruptive behaviors. It is essential for educators to use punishment sparingly, consistently, and in a fair manner to maintain a balanced and respectful learning environment.

Incorporating these operant techniques into classroom management requires thoughtful planning and consistency. Creating clear expectations, setting up reward systems, and establishing consistent consequences for misbehavior can contribute to a structured and orderly learning environment. Additionally, it is important for educators to continually assess and adjust their approach based on individual student needs, ensuring that the use of operant techniques aligns with the specific dynamics of the classroom.

Enhancement of Student Motivation through Reinforcement

Motivating students is a critical aspect of effective teaching and learning. Operant conditioning provides valuable insights into how reinforcement strategies can be employed to enhance student motivation in educational settings. By understanding the principles of reinforcement, educators can create a supportive and enriching environment that fosters intrinsic motivation and active engagement in learning.

Reinforcement serves as a powerful tool for shaping desirable behaviors and attitudes in students. Positive reinforcement involves the presentation of a rewarding stimulus following a desired behavior, leading to an increase in the likelihood of that behavior recurring. Educators can leverage positive reinforcement by acknowledging and praising students' academic achievements, effort, or positive conduct in the classroom. This approach not only boosts students' self-esteem but also cultivates a positive learning environment based on encouragement and recognition.

Negative reinforcement, often misunderstood as punishment, entails the removal of aversive stimuli upon the display of the desired behavior. In an educational context, this might involve relieving students from certain academic pressures or tasks once they have met specific academic objectives. By employing negative reinforcement judiciously, educators can help students associate their efforts with reduced stress and enhanced autonomy, fostering a sense of control over their learning journey.

In addition to traditional forms of reinforcement, educators can implement behavioral contracts and token economies to incentivize goal-oriented behavior among students. By establishing clear expectations and providing tangible rewards for meeting predetermined goals, such strategies reinforce achievement-oriented behaviors and facilitate sustained student motivation. Furthermore, incorporating choice-based reinforcement allows students to exercise autonomy in selecting preferred activities or learning paths, promoting a sense of ownership and personal investment in their education.

It is essential for educators to adapt reinforcement techniques to individual student needs and characteristics, recognizing that different students may respond divergently to various reinforcement methods. Understanding the unique preferences and motivators of each student enables educators to tailor reinforcement strategies effectively, thereby maximizing their impact on student engagement and performance.

By integrating operant conditioning principles into instructional practices, educators can cultivate a dynamic and empowering learning environment that nurtures students' intrinsic motivation, enhances their sense of competence, and fosters a lifelong love for learning.

Behavioral Issues - Punishment vs. Reinforcement

Behavioral issues are a significant concern in educational settings, often presenting challenges for educators and administrators alike. In addressing such issues, it is crucial to consider the effectiveness of punishment versus reinforcement strategies. While both approaches aim to modify behavior, they differ significantly in their impact on individuals' learning experiences and long-term outcomes. Punishment, which involves the application of aversive consequences in response to undesired behaviors, has been a historically prevalent strategy in education. However, research has shown that punitive measures may lead to negative emotional responses, resistance, and potentially exacerbate behavioral problems rather than resolve them. In contrast, reinforcement strategies, particularly positive reinforcement, offer a more constructive and sustainable approach to addressing behavioral issues. By providing positive consequences for desired behaviors, reinforcement not only motivates students but also fosters a supportive and nurturing learning environment. This approach emphasizes the importance of acknowledging and celebrating students' achievements, thus facilitating a more positive relationship between educators and learners. When implementing reinforcement strategies, it is essential to consider individual differences and tailor interventions to meet students' unique needs. This personalized approach can enhance the effectiveness of reinforcement techniques, leading to greater success in behavior modification. Moreover, the use of reinforcement aligns with principles of social-emotional learning, promoting empathy, self-regulation, and intrinsic motivation among students. While punishment may offer immediate compliance, its long-term effects on student well-being and academic engagement must be carefully weighed against the potential benefits. By understanding the distinct impact of punishment and reinforcement, educators can make informed decisions that prioritize students' holistic development and overall well-being. As we navigate the complexities of addressing behavioral issues in educational contexts, the philosophical underpinnings of punishment and reinforcement should be critically examined. It is imperative to engage in ongoing dialogue and professional development to refine and expand our repertoire of positive behavior support strategies. Ultimately, the goal is to create nurturing, inclusive learning environments that empower students to thrive academically, emotionally, and socially.

Effective Instructional Interventions

Designing effective instructional interventions requires a thorough understanding of operant conditioning principles and their application in educational settings. Educators must consider the diverse learning needs of their students, as well as the specific behaviors they aim to target for modification or enhancement. One crucial aspect is the identification of targeted behaviors that align with desired learning outcomes. This entails a detailed analysis of the antecedents and consequences associated with the behavior, allowing educators to develop targeted intervention strategies. These interventions should be tailored to individual students to ensure maximum effectiveness. Implementation of interventions involves the strategic use of reinforcement schedules and the careful consideration of timing, frequency, and magnitude of reinforcement delivery. Furthermore, educators must foster a supportive and enriching classroom environment conducive to positive behavioral change. Collaborating with other professionals, such as school psychologists or behavior analysts, can provide valuable insights and support during the intervention design phase. It is essential for educators to continuously monitor and evaluate the effectiveness of their interventions through systematic data collection and analysis. This data-driven approach allows educators to make informed decisions regarding intervention adjustments or modifications. Incorporating technology and innovative teaching methodologies can further enhance instructional interventions, providing engaging and interactive learning experiences. Lastly, ongoing professional development and training in behavior management strategies are vital for educators to continually refine their skills and stay abreast of best practices.

Implementation of Behavioral Therapy in Clinical Practice

Behavioral therapy is a widely utilized form of psychotherapy that focuses on modifying and shaping behaviors through evidence-based techniques derived from principles of operant conditioning. In clinical practice, the implementation of behavioral therapy involves a systematic and collaborative approach between the therapist, client, and often other stakeholders. The initial phase of implementing behavioral therapy in clinical practice typically involves comprehensive assessment and goal setting. This entails conducting thorough behavioral assessments, identifying maladaptive behaviors, and setting clear and measurable therapeutic goals in collaboration with the client. Subsequently, the therapist employs various behavioral techniques such as contingency management, reinforcement strategies, and behavior tracking to effectively address the identified issues. It is crucial for therapists to tailor interventions to meet the specific needs and characteristics of each client, ensuring a personalized and effective treatment approach. One of the key components of successful implementation is the establishment of a supportive therapeutic environment, where clients feel understood, valued, and empowered throughout the process. Furthermore, behavioral therapists utilize systematic desensitization, exposure therapy, and cognitive-behavioral techniques to address anxiety disorders, phobias, and other maladaptive patterns of behavior. In addition to individual therapy, behavioral therapy is also implemented in group settings, offering opportunities for social reinforcement, modeling, and peer support. Therapists need to continuously monitor and evaluate the progress of clients, adjusting interventions based on ongoing feedback and outcomes. Moreover, ethical considerations such as informed consent, confidentiality, and boundary management are integral aspects of implementing behavioral therapy in clinical practice. With the growing emphasis on evidence-based practices, therapists are encouraged to stay updated with the latest research and developments in behavioral therapy, ensuring that interventions align with the best available evidence.

Ethical Considerations in Educational and Therapeutic Contexts

In education, it is imperative to uphold the ethical standards when utilizing behavior modification techniques. This involves respecting the autonomy of students, ensuring informed consent where applicable, and maintaining confidentiality regarding individual behavioral interventions. Educators must consider the potential impact of using reinforcement and punishment on students' psychological well-being and self-esteem, aiming to promote a positive and supportive learning environment while striving to avoid the stigmatization or marginalization of any particular student.

Similarly, in the field of behavioral therapy, practitioners must adhere to a strict code of ethics to ensure the well-being of their clients. This includes obtaining informed consent, providing accurate information about the nature and purpose of the treatment, and safeguarding the privacy and confidentiality of the clients. Furthermore, it is essential for therapists to continually assess the effectiveness of behavioral interventions and be open to modifying approaches that may cause distress or discomfort to the client. This involves regularly consulting with the client to ensure they are comfortable and committed to the therapeutic process.

Ethical considerations encompass the empowerment of individuals and the promotion of their autonomy. Both in educational and therapeutic contexts, it is vital to involve students and clients in the decision-making process related to their behavioral goals and interventions. This collaborative approach not only fosters a sense of ownership and responsibility but also mitigates the risk of coercion or imposition of interventions against the individual's will.

Another significant ethical consideration revolves around the use of aversive stimuli and punishment techniques. Professionals must carefully weigh the potential benefits against the risks and ethical implications of employing such measures. It is essential to evaluate whether alternative, less intrusive methods can achieve the desired behavioral outcomes before resorting to punitive measures. Additionally, practitioners should continuously monitor and re-evaluate the appropriateness of using punishment, considering the long-term impact on the individual's well-being.

Overall, ethical considerations in educational and therapeutic applications of operant conditioning are paramount in upholding the dignity, autonomy, and well-being of the individuals involved. Practitioners and educators must integrate ethical awareness and sensitivity into their decision-making processes, striving to cultivate environments that promote growth, respect, and ethical integrity.

CRITICISMS TO OPERANT CONDITIONING

Philosophical Objections

Operant conditioning, as an approach to understanding and modifying behavior, has faced considerable philosophical objections since its inception. One of the primary criticisms pertains to the reductionist nature of behaviorist theories, including operant conditioning. Critics argue that the exclusive focus on observable behavior neglects the richness of human experience, consciousness, and subjective phenomena. This reductionist stance is seen as overly simplistic, failing to account for the complexities of human behavior and cognition. Furthermore, some philosophers argue that behaviorism, including operant conditioning, overlooks the intrinsic value of free will and autonomy in the shaping of individual actions and choices. By emphasizing external stimuli and environmental factors, behaviorism is perceived as downplaying the significance of internal processes, decision-making, and personal agency. Another philosophical objection revolves around the deterministic implications of operant conditioning. Critics contend that the deterministic nature of behaviorism undermines notions of individual responsibility and accountability. The idea that behaviors are solely shaped by reinforcement and punishment mechanisms raises concerns about the potential devaluation of personal autonomy and moral autonomy. Additionally, critics argue that the overtly mechanistic view of behavior underestimates the interconnectedness of human experience and the nuanced interplay of biological, psychological, and social factors. This oversimplified perspective diminishes the tapestry of human existence, leading to a reductive portrayal of individuals as mere products of conditioning. Lastly, opponents of behaviorism raise concerns about the ethical implications of using reinforcement and punishment to modify behavior. They question the moral justifiability of manipulating behavior through external contingencies, particularly when considering issues of coercion, consent, and respect for individual dignity. These philosophical objections highlight the need for a more comprehensive and multidimensional framework for understanding human behavior, one that integrates cognitive, emotional, and existential dimensions beyond strict behavioral contingencies.

Ethical Considerations

As with any form of behavior modification, ethical principles must guide the implementation of operant conditioning techniques. One primary concern revolves around the potential for coercion and manipulation of individuals through the use of reinforcement and punishment. This raises questions about consent, autonomy, and the potential for psychological harm. Practitioners and researchers in behavior analysis must navigate these ethical challenges with careful consideration for the well-being and rights of the individuals involved.

The use of operant conditioning raises questions about the equitable distribution of resources and opportunities. Concerns may arise regarding fairness and justice, particularly in educational and therapeutic settings where reinforcement strategies are employed. It is essential to address issues of access, equality, and the potential for reinforcing or perpetuating societal inequalities.

Another critical ethical consideration pertains to the transparency and accountability of those implementing operant conditioning interventions. Practitioners must uphold high standards of professionalism, ensuring that their actions are aligned with ethical guidelines and legal regulations. This involves obtaining informed consent, maintaining confidentiality, and continually monitoring and evaluating the impact of interventions on individuals' well-being.

In addition to ethical considerations related to the application of operant conditioning, there are broader societal implications to contemplate. The use of behavior modification techniques can influence social norms, values, and perceptions of personal agency. Ethical reflection is needed to understand the implications of promoting certain behaviors through reinforcement and addressing the potential unintended consequences of shaping behavior in specific ways.

Limitations in Complexity and Scope

In the field of operant conditioning, a significant limitation that this theory has faced lies in the oversimplification of human behavior, as proposed by critics. While operant conditioning provides a valuable framework for understanding and modifying behavior, it may overlook the interplay of genetic, cognitive, and environmental factors that contribute to individual actions. This simplification could lead to a reductionist view of human behavior, neglecting the richness and depth of human experience and decision-making processes. Moreover, it may disregard the influence of cultural norms, societal expectations, and personal values on behavioral outcomes.

Another crucial aspect is the scope of behavior that operant conditioning can effectively address. While it has demonstrated success in shaping observable behaviors, critics argue that it may struggle to account for internal states such as emotions, thoughts, and attitudes. The emphasis on external manifestations of behavior might overshadow the underlying internal processes that significantly impact an individual's actions. Furthermore, the capacity of operant conditioning to address complex, multifaceted behaviors, especially those influenced by abstract constructs such as identity formation and moral reasoning, remains a subject of debate.

Additionally, the limited scope of operant conditioning becomes evident when considering the transfer of learning across different contexts and situations. Critics contend that while operant conditioning may effectively modify behavior within controlled settings, its efficacy in promoting enduring behavioral change in varied real-world environments is uncertain. This raises concerns about the generalizability and maintenance of learned behaviors over time, particularly in dynamic and unpredictable situations.

Furthermore, the application of operant conditioning in addressing deeply ingrained behavioral patterns or psychological disorders may encounter challenges due to the nature of these issues, necessitating a more comprehensive approach.

In addressing these limitations, it becomes imperative to acknowledge the inherent complexities and contextual nuances associated with human behavior. Recognizing the multifaceted nature of behavior and incorporating insights from diverse disciplines such as psychology, sociology, and anthropology can enrich the understanding of behavior modification. Embracing a holistic perspective that encompasses both observable behaviors and internal processes enables a more comprehensive and nuanced approach towards behavior change.

Cultural and Contextual Variability

The influence of social and cultural factors on behavior presents a significant challenge to the universality of operant conditioning principles. Cultural and contextual variability refers to the understanding that behaviors, reinforcements, and punishments may hold different meanings and significance across various cultural norms and societal contexts.

Cultural and contextual considerations impact the identification and interpretation of reinforcing and punishing stimuli. Cultural norms play a crucial role in defining desirable and undesirable behaviors, shaping the types of reinforcers and punishers that hold relevance within a specific cultural milieu. Furthermore, variations in family structures, social hierarchies, and community values contribute to the complexity of behavioral dynamics.

The challenges of applying operant conditioning techniques across diverse cultures are further compounded by the diverse beliefs about individual agency and autonomy. Some cultures may prioritize collective harmony over individual independence, leading to distinct perspectives on behavior regulation and modification. The value systems and belief structures within a culture influence the conceptualization of behavioral change and the acceptability of various reinforcement and punishment strategies.

Cultural and contextual variability affects the generalization and transfer of learned behaviors. What is considered appropriate or effective reinforcement in one cultural setting may not necessarily yield similar outcomes in another. Consequently, practitioners and researchers must navigate the intricacies of cultural sensitivity and contextual adaptability when implementing operant conditioning principles.

Additionally, the consideration of cultural and contextual influences offers insights into the ethical dimensions of behavior modification. Ensuring that interventions align with culturally sensitive and contextually relevant practices is essential for promoting respect and inclusivity in behavioral interventions. Sensitivity to cultural diversity is imperative in addressing the needs and perspectives of individuals from varied cultural backgrounds.

Alternative Perspectives on Behavior Modification

In examining alternative perspectives on behavior modification, it becomes evident that various theoretical frameworks offer differing explanations for human behavior and alternative approaches to intervention. One such perspective is the cognitive-behavioral approach, which integrates elements of cognitive psychology with behaviorism. This perspective emphasizes the role of internal mental processes in shaping behavior, acknowledging the influence of thoughts, beliefs, and perceptions on an individual's actions. Proponents of this approach argue that by addressing maladaptive thought patterns and cognitive distortions, meaningful changes in behavior can be effectively achieved.

Another alternative perspective is the humanistic approach, which places emphasis on the subjective experience and self-actualization of individuals. Humanistic psychologists argue that behavior cannot be understood solely through observable stimuli and responses, but rather must be seen in the context of an individual's unique perceptions, motivations, and values. This approach advocates for a client-centered, empathic approach to behavior change, focusing on personal growth and fulfillment.

In addition, the psychodynamic perspective offers an alternative lens through which behavior modification can be understood. Rooted in the theories of Sigmund Freud and later psychodynamic theorists, this approach posits that behavior is heavily influenced by unconscious drives, conflicts, and early life experiences. Proponents of this perspective advocate for in-depth exploration of the unconscious mind and unresolved emotional wounds as a means of bringing about lasting behavioral change.

The sociocultural perspective highlights the impact of social and cultural factors on behavior. This perspective asserts that behavior is profoundly shaped by societal norms, cultural values, and social structures. It calls for a consideration of broader contextual influences in understanding and modifying behavior, recognizing the interconnectedness between individuals and their social environments.

Empirical Challenges and Counter-Evidence

One of the primary empirical challenges that operant conditioning has encountered pertains to the consistency and predictability of operant conditioning across diverse contexts and individuals. While the principles of reinforcement and punishment have been extensively studied in controlled settings, their generalizability to real-world scenarios remains a topic of contention. Studies have shown that various factors, including individual differences and environmental influences, can significantly impact the effectiveness of operant conditioning techniques. Moreover, the temporal dynamics of behavior change and the presence of confounding variables pose additional challenges to establishing a causal relationship between stimuli and responses. Furthermore, the accumulation of counter-evidence from experimental studies calls for a critical evaluation of the underlying assumptions of operant conditioning. Researchers have documented instances where behavior modification techniques based on operant principles have yielded inconsistent results or failed to produce enduring changes in behavior. These findings underscore the need for a nuanced understanding of the boundary conditions and limitations of operant conditioning. Additionally, advances in neuroscientific research have shed light on the neural mechanisms underlying behavior and cognition, prompting a reevaluation of the simplistic stimulus-response framework proposed by operant conditioning. Evidence suggesting the interplay of cognitive processes, emotional states, and motivational factors in shaping behavior challenges the reductionist nature of operant principles. Integrating these findings into the discourse surrounding operant conditioning enriches our understanding of human behavior and provides avenues for refining existing theoretical frameworks.

The Role of Cognition and Motivation

Cognitive elements such as perception, memory, decision-making, and problem-solving significantly influence how individuals respond to reinforcement and punishment. Understanding these cognitive mechanisms is crucial for a comprehensive comprehension of behavior modification. Moreover, motivation acts as a driving force behind behavior and plays a pivotal role in operant conditioning. Intrinsic motivation, extrinsic motivation, and the complexities of individual preferences and desires greatly impact the effectiveness of reinforcement strategies. We explore how intrinsic motivators, such as autonomy and mastery, can foster sustainable behavioral change, while external motivators, like rewards and punishments, may exert limited and short-term effects.

The reciprocal relationship between cognition and motivation warrants thorough consideration. The cognitive processes involved in evaluating potential rewards and punishments, weighing consequences, and making decisions are deeply intertwined with motivational states. This dynamic interaction between cognition and motivation demonstrates the multidimensional nature of behavior modification.

We also address the implications of cognitive and motivational factors for practical applications of operant conditioning. By integrating cognitive-behavioral approaches and motivational enhancement techniques, practitioners can design more tailored and effective behavior intervention programs. Recognizing the individual differences in cognitive styles and motivational orientations empowers educators, therapists, and behavior analysts to customize interventions that resonate with the unique needs and aspirations of each learner or client.

Recent Developments in Criticism

In recent years, the field of operant conditioning has faced a wave of new criticisms and challenges that have sparked extensive debate and further exploration. One notable development is the increasing attention to the cultural and contextual considerations that shape behavior and learning processes. Scholars and practitioners have emphasized the need to acknowledge the diversity of human experiences and recognize the influence of socio-cultural factors on behavioral patterns. This shift has led to more nuanced discussions about the generalizability of operant conditioning principles across different populations and settings.

Another significant aspect of recent criticism pertains to the ethical dimensions of behavior modification techniques derived from operant conditioning. With growing awareness of individual rights and autonomy, there has been a heightened scrutiny of the potential risks and unintended consequences associated with the application of reinforcement and punishment strategies. Ethicists and professionals have called for the refinement of ethical guidelines and safeguards to ensure that behavioral interventions uphold principles of respect, fairness, and welfare.

Advances in cognitive psychology and neuroscience have brought about a deeper understanding of the interplay between cognition, emotion, and behavior, challenging the simplistic stimulus-response framework often associated with operant conditioning. This has spurred ongoing debates on the integration of cognitive elements into behavior analysis and the implications for refining intervention strategies.

A particularly contentious area of recent development centers on the resurgence of interest in alternative approaches to behavior modification, including humanistic and person-centered models that prioritize individual agency, personal growth, and holistic well-being. Proponents of these perspectives argue for a more comprehensive and humanizing stance toward understanding and influencing behavior, diverging from the behaviorist roots of operant conditioning.

Emerging empirical research has also raised questions about the robustness and universal applicability of traditional operant conditioning principles. Studies exploring the complexities of human motivation, self-regulation, and interpersonal dynamics have complicated the deterministic view of behavior change and highlighted the need for a more dynamic, multidimensional approach.

COMPARISON WITH OTHER LEARNING THEORIES

Social Learning Theory

Social learning theory, pioneered by Albert Bandura, presents a compelling framework for understanding the role of observational learning in human behavior. At the core of this theory lies the premise that individuals learn not only through direct reinforcement or punishment but also by observing and imitating others within their social environment.

A central tenet of social learning theory is the concept of modeling, where individuals emulate the behaviors exhibited by others, known as models, whom they perceive as credible, competent, or prestigious. Bandura's famous Bobo doll experiment exemplified the power of modeling, demonstrating how children imitated aggressive behaviors witnessed in adults. This sheds light on the influential role of media, family members, peers, and societal figures in shaping behavioral patterns through observational learning.

The theory elucidates the significance of vicarious reinforcement, wherein individuals observe the consequences of others' actions and adjust their behavior accordingly. By witnessing others being rewarded or punished for specific behaviors, individuals undergo a cognitive process of internalizing these outcomes, thereby influencing their future conduct. From a broader perspective, this mechanism has profound implications in diverse settings, including education, workplace dynamics, and social interactions.

Social learning theory emphasizes the crucial interplay between cognition and behavior. It underscores the cognitive processes involved in attention, retention, reproduction, and motivation, as essential components of observational learning. This integrative approach highlights the complex mental operations underlying the acquisition and manifestation of behaviors observed in others, offering a nuanced understanding of human learning dynamics.

Critically, the theory accentuates the role of self-efficacy in determining the likelihood of individuals to engage in observed behaviors. By assessing their own capabilities to successfully execute a behavior, people are more inclined to replicate actions they perceive as attainable, reinforcing the bidirectional relationship between cognitive factors and behavioral enactment.

Cognitive Learning Theory

Cognitive learning theory is a comprehensive framework that focuses on the internal mental processes involved in learning, as opposed to purely external stimulus-response associations. At its core, cognitive learning theory emphasizes the role of mental structures and processes in shaping human behavior and cognition. Unlike behavioral theories that center on observable behaviors, cognitive theory delves into how individuals encode, process, and retrieve information, and how these mental activities influence learning and behavior.

One of the fundamental principles of cognitive learning theory is the concept of schema, which refers to an individual's organized knowledge structure. Schemas encompass concepts, categories, and relationships, influencing how new information is interpreted and integrated with existing knowledge. This departure from behaviorist views emphasizes the importance of prior knowledge, perception, and thought processes in shaping learning outcomes.

Cognitive learning theory places significant emphasis on memory processes and information processing models. It explores the stages of memory, including sensory memory, short-term memory, and long-term memory, shedding light on how information is retained and utilized over time. Additionally, the theory delves into the cognitive processes involved in problem-solving, decision-making, and reasoning, shedding light on the intricacies of human thought.

Contrasting cognitive learning theory with other paradigms, such as behaviorism and constructivism, reveals distinctive perspectives on the nature of learning. While behaviorism downplays the role of internal mental processes, focusing on external stimuli and responses, cognitive theory highlights the active role of the learner's mind. Similarly, constructivism emphasizes the learner's active participation in constructing knowledge, aligning with cognitive theory's recognition of the learner's proactive engagement in the learning process.

The integration of cognitive neuroscience has enriched our understanding of cognitive learning processes, unraveling the neural underpinnings of memory, attention, and decision-making. The interdisciplinary nature of cognitive learning theory incorporates insights from psychology, neuroscience, linguistics, and artificial intelligence, offering a multidimensional perspective on learning.

Humanist Learning Theories

Humanist learning theories emphasize the significance of individual experiences, emotions, and personal agency in the process of learning. Stemming from humanistic psychology, these theories prioritize the holistic development of individuals, focusing on their emotional and social well-being alongside cognitive growth. In contrast to behaviorist and cognitivist perspectives, humanist theories, such as those proposed by Carl Rogers and Abraham Maslow, underscore the innate desire for self-actualization and the importance of human potential in learning. Central to humanist theories is the concept of learner-centered education, which advocates for personalized, student-driven approaches that recognize the uniqueness of each learner. Rather than adopting a standardized or uniform method of instruction, humanist learning theories endorse nurturing an environment that honors diversity and encourages self-exploration. Key principles of humanist theories include unconditional positive regard, empathetic understanding, and the encouragement of creativity and self-expression. By emphasizing individualism in learning, these theories aim to promote a sense of autonomy and intrinsic motivation within learners, inspiring them to take ownership of their educational journeys. Humanist approaches also stress the significance of interpersonal relationships and collaborative learning environments, fostering a sense of community and mutual respect. Furthermore, in embracing the whole person, humanist theories acknowledge the interconnectedness of social, emotional, and cognitive aspects in the learning process. This integration fosters a more comprehensive educational experience that acknowledges the multifaceted nature of human development. As educators and researchers continue to explore the implications of humanist learning theories, there remains ongoing discourse on the practical implementation of these principles in diverse educational settings. Balancing the ideals of individualism with the structural demands of formal education presents challenges, yet the potential benefits of promoting self-directed, compassionate, and meaningful learning experiences are increasingly recognized.

Constructivist Approaches

Constructivism is a pedagogical philosophy that emphasizes the active role of the learner in constructing their understanding of the world. This approach asserts that learners build knowledge and understanding through meaningful experiences, reflection, and cognitive processes. Rather than passively receiving information, learners actively engage with new ideas, concepts, and skills, integrating them into their existing knowledge framework.

Central to constructivist approaches is the notion that learning is influenced by social and cultural contexts. As such, educators utilizing this approach often design learning environments that encourage collaboration, discussion, and inquiry-based activities. By fostering interactions with peers, instructors, and real-world applications, learners can explore diverse perspectives and negotiate meanings, enhancing their construction of knowledge.

One key implication of constructivist approaches is the emphasis on metacognition and self-regulated learning. Learners are encouraged to reflect on their thinking processes, monitor their understanding, and regulate their learning strategies. This metacognitive awareness fosters autonomy and independence in learning, equipping individuals with tools to manage their own learning experiences effectively.

Constructivism underscores the value of authentic tasks and real-world problem-solving. By presenting learners with challenging, open-ended problems, educators promote critical thinking, creativity, and the application of knowledge in practical contexts. This approach cultivates skills beyond rote memorization, nurturing a deeper understanding of subject matter and its relevance to actual situations.

Critics of the constructivist approach argue that it may not always align with standardized assessments and traditional educational structures. However, proponents highlight that constructivism better prepares learners for the complexities of the modern world, where adaptability, creativity, and lifelong learning are highly valued.

In today's digital age, technology has also influenced constructivist practices, offering immersive simulations, interactive platforms, and collaborative tools that augment learner engagement and exploration. Integrating technological resources with constructivist principles can provide dynamic learning experiences that resonate with contemporary learners.

Information Processing Models

Information processing models form a fascinating framework for understanding how individuals perceive, interpret, and respond to stimuli. These models propose that human cognition mirrors the functioning of a computer, with incoming information processed through various stages before producing a behavioral response. The section delves into the intricacies of cognitive architectures and mechanisms, shedding light on the interplay of sensory memory, working memory, and long-term memory in shaping human learning processes. By exploring the concepts of attention, encoding, and retrieval within this framework, readers gain valuable insights into the complex underpinnings of cognitive function. Moreover, the section examines the role of executive functions, such as cognitive control and decision-making, in mediating learning outcomes and adaptive behavior. It also discusses the influence of cognitive load and mental resources on information processing, elucidating how factors like multitasking and stress can impact learning efficiency. Furthermore, the section scrutinizes the connectionist models and parallel distributed processing systems, highlighting their contributions to understanding how knowledge is represented and accessed in the human mind. Emphasizing the significance of metacognition and self-regulation, it outlines the strategies individuals employ to monitor and optimize their cognitive processes, thereby enhancing their learning experiences.

Integrative Perspectives

In the field of educational psychology, the notion of syncretism plays a pivotal role in understanding the interconnectedness and compatibility of various learning theories. When evaluating syncretism in learning theories, it is essential to consider how different theoretical frameworks can be integrated to create a comprehensive understanding of human learning and behavior. This integrative perspective involves examining the commonalities and divergences among learning theories, emphasizing the mutual influence and overlap that exists between them.

One approach to evaluating the syncretism in learning theories is through a comparative analysis of foundational principles and underlying assumptions. By scrutinizing the core tenets of different learning theories, such as behaviorism, cognitivism, and constructivism, educators and researchers can elucidate their shared elements and identify opportunities for integration. Moreover, this process facilitates a deeper appreciation of the multifaceted nature of learning, acknowledging that diverse perspectives contribute to a more holistic comprehension of educational phenomena.

An integrative perspective requires a nuanced examination of how the practical applications of distinct learning theories intersect and complement each other in real-world contexts. Educators are confronted with the challenge of crafting pedagogical approaches that draw from multiple theoretical frameworks to cater to the diverse needs and learning styles of students. By assessing the pragmatic implications of integrating learning theories, educators can cultivate dynamic instructional strategies that harness the strengths of each theory while mitigating their respective limitations.

Another facet of evaluating syncretism in learning theories involves considering the developmental and sociocultural dimensions of learning. Recognizing that learning occurs within complex socio-environmental systems, an integrative perspective encompasses an exploration of how various learning theories address the interaction between individual cognitive processes and external influences. By embracing a holistic understanding of learning that incorporates sociocultural and contextual factors, educators can foster more inclusive and culturally responsive instructional practices.

This integrative perspective emphasizes the need for interdisciplinary collaboration and dialogue among scholars and practitioners from diverse fields. By transcending disciplinary boundaries and engaging in cross-disciplinary discourse, educators and researchers can cultivate a rich tapestry of ideas and insights that transcend the confines of singular learning theories. This collaborative endeavor fosters a symbiotic relationship among different theoretical paradigms, enabling the emergence of novel frameworks that integrate the wisdom of various disciplines.

Pragmatic Applications

Exhibiting a deep understanding of various learning theories serves as a cornerstone for designing effective educational strategies and interventions. The pragmatic applications of these theories extend across diverse educational settings, catering to the individual needs and learning styles of students. By drawing on the insights provided by classical conditioning, educators can devise behavior modification plans that target specific responses in students. Meanwhile, social learning theory emphasizes the crucial role of observational learning, prompting educators to create collaborative and interactive learning environments where students can observe and emulate positive behaviors.

Cognitive learning theory underscores the significance of mental processes such as attention, memory, and problem-solving, guiding educators to develop instructional methods that stimulate critical thinking and information retention. Humanist learning theories, with their focus on self-actualization and personal growth, inspire educators to nurture an environment that fosters creativity, autonomy, and respect for individual differences, thus promoting holistic development. Similarly, constructivist approaches advocate for learner-centered exploration and discovery, encouraging educators to facilitate active learning experiences and promote the construction of knowledge through hands-on activities and real-world applications.

Information processing models provide valuable insights into how learners perceive, encode, store, and retrieve information, leading educators to adopt strategies that optimize cognitive processing and memory consolidation. Integrative perspectives enable educators to synthesize the strengths of multiple theories to create a comprehensive, adaptive, and inclusive approach to education, ensuring that diverse learners receive tailored support and opportunities for growth. By honing an understanding of the practical implications across these varied theories, educators are equipped to employ a multidimensional approach in their teaching practices, accommodating the multifaceted needs of learners and fostering an enriching educational experience.

Overarching this discussion of practical applications is the recognition that leveraging a spectrum of learning theories enhances pedagogical effectiveness, allowing educators to tailor their practices to meet the unique requirements of their students. Through the conscientious integration of these theoretical contributions, educators can design instructional approaches that resonate with the diverse learning preferences and aptitudes of their students, thereby cultivating an inclusive, engaging, and impactful learning environment.

FUTURE DIRECTIONS IN OPERANT CONDITIONING

Innovative Methodologies and Technologies

In the field of operant conditioning, innovative methodologies and cutting-edge technologies have significantly transformed the way researchers study and apply behavioral principles. One notable development is the integration of advanced data analytics and machine learning algorithms to analyze complex behavioral patterns and predict outcomes with greater precision. These computational approaches allow for the exploration of large datasets, unveiling nuanced relationships between environmental variables and behavioral responses. Moreover, virtual reality (VR) and augmented reality (AR) technologies have revolutionized the simulation of real-world environments for behavioral experiments, enabling researchers to create controlled settings that mimic naturalistic conditions. By immersing subjects in interactive virtual scenarios, scientists can observe and manipulate behaviors in a highly controlled manner, offering insights that were previously unattainable. Additionally, the use of biofeedback devices and wearable sensors has opened up new avenues for real-time monitoring of physiological and behavioral markers, facilitating a deeper understanding of the underlying mechanisms of operant conditioning. These tools provide invaluable objective measures, allowing researchers to capture subtle changes in responses and tailor interventions more effectively. Furthermore, advancements in neuroimaging techniques, such as functional magnetic resonance imaging (fMRI) and electroencephalography (EEG), have fostered a greater understanding of the neural correlates of operant behavior. By elucidating the brain-behavior relationships, these methodologies offer profound insights into the cognitive processes underpinning operant conditioning paradigms. The integration of robotics and automation has also streamlined the implementation of operant conditioning protocols, enhancing experimental precision and reproducibility while minimizing human error. Through the seamless integration of these innovative methodologies and technologies, the field of operant conditioning continues to push the boundaries of knowledge, shedding light on the dynamics of behavior-environment interactions and paving the way for transformative applications in diverse domains including psychology, neuroscience, education, and rehabilitation.

Neuroscientific Advances in Operant Conditioning

Recent years have seen a surge of interest in exploring the neuroscientific underpinnings of operant conditioning. Researchers are delving into the workings of the brain to understand how different neurological processes contribute to learning and behavior modification. One key focus area is the role of neurotransmitters, such as dopamine and serotonin, in shaping reinforcement mechanisms. Studies have elucidated the complex interplay between these neurotransmitters and the neural circuits involved in reward processing, shedding light on the neurological basis of operant behavior.

Advancements in neuroimaging techniques, such as functional magnetic resonance imaging (fMRI) and electroencephalography (EEG), have enabled researchers to observe the brain's activity in real time during operant conditioning tasks. This has provided unprecedented insights into how specific brain regions, such as the prefrontal cortex and the limbic system, contribute to the learning process. By mapping the neural correlates of operant behavior, scientists are uncovering the neural signatures associated with reinforcement, punishment, and decision-making, offering a window into the inner workings of the mind.

Another exciting avenue of research involves the intersection of neuroscience and technology in the development of neuromodulation techniques. Non-invasive methods, such as transcranial magnetic stimulation (TMS) and transcranial direct current stimulation (tDCS), are being explored for their potential to modulate neural activity and enhance operant conditioning outcomes. These approaches hold promise for optimizing learning and behavioral interventions by directly targeting neural circuits implicated in operant processes.

Studies investigating the impact of environmental enrichment and sensory stimulation on neural plasticity have highlighted the interconnectedness of environmental factors and neurological adaptations underlying operant conditioning. A deeper understanding of how the environment interacts with neural processes opens up new avenues for designing enriched learning environments that promote adaptive behaviors through targeted sensory experiences.

Cross-Disciplinary Approaches and Collaborations

The advancement of operant conditioning has been greatly facilitated by the integration of insights and methodologies from a wide range of disciplines. Collaborations between behavioral scientists, neuroscientists, computer engineers, and practitioners in various fields have led to innovative approaches and a deeper understanding of behavior modification. By leveraging expertise from different domains, researchers have been able to explore the complex interplay between cognitive processes, neural mechanisms, and environmental influences on operant behavior.

In the field of neuroscience, partnerships with cognitive psychologists and neurobiologists have provided valuable insights into the neural circuits and neurotransmitter systems involved in reinforcement and punishment processes. These collaborations have not only enriched our understanding of the underlying neural mechanisms but have also opened up new avenues for targeted interventions and treatments for behavioral disorders.

The intersection of operant conditioning with digital technology has given rise to exciting possibilities for real-time data collection, analysis, and intervention delivery. Here, collaborations with experts in human-computer interaction, data science, and artificial intelligence have yielded novel tools and platforms for personalized behavior modification programs. These cross-disciplinary efforts have the potential to revolutionize the way operant conditioning is applied in educational settings, clinical therapies, and everyday life.

Beyond the traditional boundaries of psychology and neuroscience, collaborations with experts in fields such as economics, public policy, and sociology have enabled a more comprehensive exploration of the societal impacts of operant conditioning principles. By integrating behavioral economic theories and sociocultural perspectives, researchers have gained a better understanding of how social norms, economic incentives, and policy frameworks can influence the effectiveness of operant conditioning interventions at a population level.

The synergistic effects of cross-disciplinary collaborations extend beyond the field of research and theory-building. These partnerships have also paved the way for the development of evidence-based practices that are more responsive to the complex and dynamic nature of human behavior. By fostering dialogue and knowledge exchange across diverse disciplines, the field of operant conditioning stands to benefit from a rich tapestry of ideas and approaches that can address multifaceted challenges in promoting adaptive behaviors and well-being.

Operant Conditioning in Digital Environments

The application of operant conditioning principles in digital environments represents a significant area of interest and innovation within the field of behavioral research. With the ubiquity of technology and its integration into various aspects of daily life, understanding how operant conditioning can be leveraged in digital contexts is vital for addressing a wide range of behavioral challenges and opportunities. The potential for digitally mediated operant conditioning opens up new possibilities for behavior modification, skill acquisition, and intervention strategies. In educational settings, digital platforms provide a rich landscape for implementing personalized reinforcement schedules, adaptive learning systems, and real-time feedback mechanisms based on operant conditioning principles. By integrating gamification elements and interactive interfaces, educators and researchers can create engaging environments that facilitate effective shaping of behaviors and skill development. Moreover, in the field of digital health and wellness applications, operant conditioning techniques can be utilized to promote adherence to therapeutic regimens, encourage healthy lifestyle choices, and address problematic behaviors such as addiction or compulsive habits. The use of wearable devices, mobile apps, and virtual reality simulations allows for continuous monitoring and targeted delivery of reinforcements, thereby enhancing the efficacy of behavior change interventions. However, the proliferation of operant conditioning strategies in digital environments also raises ethical considerations regarding data privacy, consent, and potential misuse of behavioral influence. As algorithms and AI technologies become more sophisticated in predicting and shaping human behavior, safeguarding against exploitation and unintended consequences becomes paramount. Furthermore, the dynamic nature of digital platforms necessitates ongoing evaluation of their impact on individual autonomy, psychological well-being, and social dynamics. Balancing the benefits of applying operant conditioning in digital environments with safeguarding ethical principles requires multidisciplinary collaboration and proactive regulatory frameworks. Continued research in this domain is essential for refining best practices, identifying potential pitfalls, and establishing guidelines for responsible implementation. As digital technologies continue to evolve, so too must our understanding of how operant conditioning can be ethically and effectively integrated into these novel contexts.

Ethical Considerations in Modern Research

As advancements in technology and methodology continue to expand the frontiers of behavioral analysis, researchers and practitioners must remain vigilant in upholding ethical standards. One of the fundamental ethical concerns involves the treatment of research subjects, whether they are humans or non-human animals. Striking a balance between scientific inquiry and respect for the well-being of subjects is crucial. This necessitates adherence to established guidelines and protocols, as well as obtaining informed consent from human participants. Additionally, utilizing non-invasive and humane methods when working with animal subjects is imperative. Furthermore, ensuring that the benefits of the research outweigh any potential harm is essential. Beyond the treatment of subjects, ethical considerations also extend to the dissemination of findings and the potential implications for society. Researchers must strive for transparency and accuracy when communicating their results, avoiding sensationalism or misrepresentation. Moreover, they should consider the broader impact of their work on individuals, communities, and cultures, particularly when exploring sensitive topics or implementing interventions. Cultural competence and sensitivity to diverse perspectives are integral components of ethical research in operant conditioning. Embracing this mindset allows for a more nuanced understanding of the implications of behavioral principles across different societal contexts. Another crucial aspect of ethical conduct involves the responsible use of data and resources. Safeguarding the privacy and confidentiality of research participants' information is non-negotiable, demanding robust data management and security measures. As technology continues to play a significant role in behavioral research, ethical considerations surrounding data collection, storage, and utilization become increasingly complex. Researchers must navigate these challenges with integrity and accountability, recognizing the potential for both positive advancements and unforeseen consequences. The evolving landscape of modern research in operant conditioning underscores the need for ongoing ethical reflection and dialogue. By prioritizing ethical considerations, the field can not only advance scientifically but also cultivate trust, credibility, and social responsibility.

Global Perspectives and Cultural Variations

One of the key considerations when examining global perspectives in operant conditioning is the cultural interpretation of behaviors and reinforcements. Different cultures may attribute varying significance to certain behaviors and stimuli. As such, what is considered reinforcing or punishing in one culture may not hold the same meaning in another. Understanding these cultural nuances is critical for effective implementation of operant conditioning techniques in diverse settings.

Cultural variations also influence the methodologies and approaches used in operant conditioning research and application. For instance, traditional Western paradigms may not seamlessly translate into non-Western contexts due to differences in social structures, values, and belief systems. Researchers and practitioners must be cognizant of these variations to ensure that operant conditioning interventions are culturally sensitive and relevant.

Exploring global perspectives allows for insight into the effectiveness of operant conditioning across different socio-economic landscapes. The accessibility and availability of reinforcements, as well as the acceptance of behavioral interventions, can vary significantly based on economic conditions and societal norms. Understanding these factors is crucial when designing tailored operant conditioning strategies that align with the specific needs of diverse populations.

Additionally, the incorporation of cultural perspectives in operant conditioning research enriches the field by fostering cross-cultural collaborations and exchange of knowledge. By acknowledging and embracing cultural diversity, researchers can develop more holistic and adaptable frameworks that resonate with varied populations worldwide.

Barriers to Implementation and Adoption

The dissemination and implementation of operant conditioning principles, despite their proven efficacy, have encountered several barriers that hinder widespread adoption across diverse professional domains. One notable challenge arises from the resistance to change and traditional practices deeply rooted in various societal and organizational cultures. This resistance often stems from a lack of understanding or misinterpretation of operant conditioning, which may lead to skepticism and reluctance to embrace new behavioral interventions.

Limited access to proper training and education on operant conditioning techniques remains a significant barrier. Professionals in fields such as education, healthcare, and organizational management may not receive adequate exposure to these methods during their formal training, rendering them less inclined to incorporate operant conditioning into their respective practices. Additionally, misconceptions about the ethical implications of behavior modification and concerns about potential negative consequences for individuals subjected to reinforcement or punishment contribute to hesitancy in adopting operant conditioning strategies.

Another critical obstacle involves the complexity of tailoring operant conditioning principles to specific cultural contexts. Cultural norms, values, and belief systems vary widely across populations, posing challenges in adapting universal behavioral interventions to address culturally diverse needs. Without careful consideration of these cultural nuances, the implementation of operant conditioning approaches may inadvertently encounter resistance or lack of acceptance from communities with distinct social and cultural backgrounds.

Financial constraints and resource limitations present practical barriers to the widespread utilization of operant conditioning methodologies. The costs associated with implementing comprehensive behavior modification programs, acquiring necessary equipment, and employing skilled professionals proficient in operant conditioning techniques can pose substantial burdens for organizations and institutions, particularly those with constrained budgets. As a result, the potential benefits of operant conditioning may remain untapped due to financial disparities and resource disparities across different sectors.

Promising Areas for Future Exploration

The field of operant conditioning continues to be a dynamic area of research and practice, with several promising areas for future exploration. One such domain is the application of operant principles in the context of virtual and augmented reality environments. As technology rapidly advances, the potential for creating immersive learning experiences that integrate operant conditioning techniques holds great promise. This includes the development of interactive simulations and adaptive training systems that can tailor reinforcement schedules to individualized learning profiles, thereby optimizing skill acquisition and retention.

Another avenue for future exploration lies in the intersection of neurobiology and operant conditioning. With advancements in neuroscience and neuroimaging techniques, researchers are gaining deeper insights into the neural mechanisms underlying operant behavior. Understanding the neural circuitry involved in reinforcement, decision-making, and learning processes can open new frontiers for targeted interventions in clinical and educational settings. Furthermore, exploring the neurobiological basis of behavioral variability and individual differences in response to reinforcement holds potential for refining and personalizing operant-based interventions.

In addition, the integration of operant conditioning with other behavioral frameworks, such as ecological psychology and complex systems theory, presents an intriguing direction for future inquiry. These interdisciplinary collaborations offer the opportunity to enrich our understanding of behavior in naturalistic contexts, offering a more holistic perspective on operant processes within complex environmental networks. By embracing a multilevel approach that considers both the individual organism and its ecological niche, new insights may emerge regarding the adaptive value and dynamics of operant behaviors across diverse ecological and social contexts.

The exploration of cultural variations and cross-cultural applications of operant principles represents an underdeveloped area ripe for investigation. Understanding how sociocultural factors shape reinforcement contingencies, motivation, and behavioral outcomes can shed light on the universality versus cultural specificity of operant processes. Comparative studies across different cultural groups can uncover valuable insights into the impact of societal norms, values, and traditions on shaping operant behaviors, thus informing culturally sensitive interventions and educational practices.

Lastly, the ethical considerations surrounding the use of operant techniques in various domains, including education, healthcare, and organizational management, demand continued attention and scrutiny in future research endeavors. Balancing the potential benefits of behavior-based interventions with concerns regarding autonomy, consent, and unintended consequences necessitates ongoing ethical reflection and oversight.

In summary, the field of operant conditioning presents numerous exciting opportunities for future exploration, spanning technological innovation, neuroscientific inquiries, interdisciplinary collaborations, cultural investigations, and ethical deliberations. Embracing these frontiers promises to enrich our understanding of behavior and expand the practical utility of operant principles in addressing complex societal challenges.

SKINNER'S 50 QUOTES ON OPERANT CONDITIONING

On Operant Conditioning and Behavior

"The consequences of an act affect the probability of its occurring again."

"Operant behavior is behavior 'controlled' by its consequences."

"A person does not act upon the world, the world acts upon him."

"Behavior is shaped and maintained by its consequences."

"We shouldn't teach great books; we should teach a love of reading."

"A failure is not always a mistake, it may simply be the best one can do under the circumstances."

"The environment determines behavior."

"What is love except another name for the use of positive reinforcement?"

"We do not choose survival; it chooses us."

"The real problem is not whether machines think but whether men do."

On Reinforcement

"Positive reinforcement is the most effective way to shape behavior."

"Reinforcement builds behavior; punishment only suppresses it."

"The strengthening of behavior which results from reinforcement is appropriately called 'conditioning'."

"If a certain kind of behavior is followed by a certain kind of consequence, the behavior is more likely to occur again."

"Punished behavior is not forgotten, it's suppressed."

"A behavior followed by a reinforcing stimulus results in an increased probability of that behavior occurring in the future."

"Reinforcement is more humane than punishment."

"The ideal of behavior modification is to reinforce behavior you want, rather than punish what you don't."

"We must make effective reinforcement available."

"We must practice the art of reinforcement with care."

On Punishment

"Punishment may work in the short run, but it has many unwanted side effects."

"The threat of punishment will not deter if reinforcement for the behavior remains."

"Punishment does not teach what to do; it only teaches what not to do."

"The consequences of punishment may be more detrimental than the behavior it seeks to suppress."

"When you punish someone, you do not change the tendency to behave in a given way. Instead, you only suppress the behavior temporarily."

On Free Will and Determinism

"Man is not free. He is not autonomous. He is controlled by the environment."

"We are not free to choose; we are shaped by reinforcement history."

"The feeling of freedom is an illusion; it is a byproduct of ignorance of the causes of behavior."

"A scientific view of man offers a way of treating human behavior as a subject matter in its own right."

"We must abandon the illusion of free will if we are to truly understand human behavior."

On Environment and Control

"The environment makes the man."

"Behavior is controlled by its consequences, and these consequences are determined by the environment."

"Control is not a dirty word. It's a necessary function of social organization."

"To control behavior, we must control the environment."

"Education is what survives when what has been learned has been forgotten."

"Society attacks early, when the individual is helpless."

"To say that a man chooses his behavior is to say that he is free to behave as he chooses. This is not so."

On Learning and Education

"Learning is a process of acquiring new behavior through reinforcement."

"Education is the establishment of behavior which will prove useful or enjoyable later."

"Good teaching is the arrangement of contingencies of reinforcement under which students learn."

"A student is not a container you have to fill, but a torch you have to light."

"We need to make learning reinforcing in and of itself."

On Scientific Method and Psychology

"Science is a way of thinking much more than it is a body of knowledge."

"Psychology must discard mentalistic explanations of behavior."

"Behaviorism is not the science of human behavior; it is the philosophy of that science."

"The analysis of behavior is not speculation; it is based on empirical evidence."

"Only by observing behavior can we discover the laws of learning."

From "Beyond Freedom and Dignity" and "Walden Two"

"We can achieve a better society through the scientific control of behavior."

"In a properly designed culture, there is no need for coercion."

"A utopian society is not a fantasy; it is a behavioral experiment."

www.ingramcontent.com/pod-product-compliance
Lightning Source LLC
LaVergne TN
LVHW022042200926
848481LV00003B/749